WARTIME WRITINGS

OTHER BOOKS BY ANTOINE DE SAINT-EXUPÉRY

Flight to Arras
The Little Prince
Night Flight
Southern Mail
Wind, Sand and Stars
The Wisdom of the Sands
Airman's Odyssey

ANTOINE DE SAINT-EXUPÉRY

WARTIME WRITINGS 1939–1944

Translated by Norah Purcell

*With an Introduction
by Anne Morrow Lindbergh*

A Harvest/HBJ Book
HARCOURT BRACE JOVANOVICH, PUBLISHERS
San Diego   New York   London

HBJ

Library of Congress Cataloging-in-Publication Data
Saint-Exupéry, Antoine de, 1900–1944.
Wartime writings, 1939–1944.
Translation of: Ecrits de guerre, 1939–1944.
Includes bibliographical references.
1. Saint-Exupéry, Antoine de, 1900–1944—Biography.
2. Saint-Exupéry, Antoine de, 1900–1944—Translations,
English. 3. Authors, French—20th century—Biography.
4. Air pilots, Military—France—Biography. 5. World
War, 1939–1945—Personal narratives, French. I. Title.
PQ2637.A274Z46513 1986 848'.91209 [B] 85-30566
ISBN 0-15-194680-9
ISBN 0-15-694740-4 (pbk.)

Designed by Kate Nichols
Printed in the United States of America

First Harvest/HBJ edition 1990

A B C D E

Contents

Note from the French Publisher

The pages we present here are the miscellaneous writings of a man who went to war, then was forced into inaction, and finally returned to die on a military flying mission.

Some of these writings were published in journals or newspapers now no longer available. Many are unpublished. These are mostly letters, but also drafts, jottings cast aside, radio broadcasts, or bulletins to the American press.

We have arranged this material in chronological order, adding only brief explanations. The chronology in fact begins shortly before the declaration of war. We wanted to show Saint-Exupéry in his activities, thoughts, and contacts during the summer of 1939.

We wish to thank the owners of unpublished texts by Saint-Exupéry who very kindly put them at our disposal.

The letters mentioned as "Letter to X" are messages to persons who do not wish their names to appear.

These documents were collected and arranged by Nicole and Louis Evrard.

Introduction

Antoine de Saint-Exupéry, pioneer mail pilot on one of the world's earliest lines; war pilot in World War II; and author of several best-selling books, is remembered in the United States today chiefly for his small haunting "fairy tale"—supposedly written for children—*The Little Prince*. The first books of flying adventure have gone into many editions and are still selling in paperback. They will remain the classic literature of early aviation, but they are not limited to one period or one profession.

In the last fifty years flying has changed radically, but human values have an enduring importance. *Wind, Sand and Stars*, an epic account of the author's travels through skies and over earth, reflects a point of view that is astonishingly timeless. Written before the war, before rocket propulsion, before man traveled to the moon, the book gave a farsighted plea, repeated later by many others. "I wrote *Wind, Sand and Stars*," Saint-Exupéry states, "in order to tell men passionately that they were all inhabitants of the same planet, passengers on the same ship."

In 1939, shortly after the American publication of *Wind, Sand and Stars*, my husband and I were fortunate enough to meet Saint-Exupéry while he was in New York. We were then living on Long Island Sound. My diary vividly recalls the details of that radiant August weekend, when carefree conversation sparked against storm clouds of impending war.

Earlier that month we had received through my publisher a letter from Saint-Exupéry, containing a preface he had written for the French translation of my book, *Listen! The Wind*. The letter explained that he had agreed to write a polite one-page preface, in honor of the Lindbergh name, before reading the book. But after reading it on the boat crossing the Atlantic, he cabled the publishers that he needed to say more and had written nine pages, which he enclosed.

As my diary* records on August 4, I found the preface intensely beautiful and was moved "not only with the importance he attaches to the book and his analysis of it . . . but I am startled by what he has seen of me. The note says he would like to meet me."

August 5. "We call Saint-Exupéry. He speaks 'pas un mot' of English. I have to talk to him—what a prospect! Yes, he would be delighted to come out for dinner and the night." C. leaves for upstate New York and will pick him up on his way home. At three he calls and says he cannot make it. Will I pick up Saint-Exupéry?

"I tear into town, rather cross to be late." At the hotel they say that M. Saint-Exupéry is in the bar. He apears—a big man, stooping slightly and somewhat bald—not really good-looking— "an inscrutable sort of face, almost Slavic in its solidity and inscrutability, his eyes turn up at the corners a little.

"Oh—it's *that* man, is it? I think, with a confused dream feeling that I have seen him often before—met him, even. I

---

* Published as *War Within and Without* (New York: Harcourt Brace Jovanovich, 1980).

recognize him immediately. I apologize for being late and we go across to the car and start out. We hardly get around the block when the car stalls and will not start again. And all this time we are talking at top speed—with a kind of intensity that precluded any attention to practical details." He is talking about my book and pulls the preface out of his pocket. I am distracted, trying to talk French, always an effort, and talking to a taxi driver and trying to explain in French and then in English what was wrong with the car.

"But perhaps you do not like the preface?" he says at some point.

"Oh, yes—yes!" I try to reassure him. I was astonished at his modesty about his writing and his anxiety lest I had not understood it all.

And so the weekend went on, chiefly in conversation. My husband and Saint-Exupéry compared notes on the early days of aviation. They talked of the current crisis: Germany's power, England's next move, France's inherent strength. Breaking through the surface conversation, the deeper concern of Saint-Exupéry's books emerged: the place of the machine in modern life. He was "optimistic that man would come out on top of the machine—use it as a tool for greater spiritual ends." He spoke also of danger and solitude being the two factors that go to form a man's character. I noted in my diary: "There is a kind of mountaintop austerity about him that reminds me of a monk, dedicated to something—what?"

And yet his sense of play enlivened the weekend: doing card tricks at a friend's house, obviously enjoying in a childlike way our bafflement. Sitting at supper on our porch, when I took a June bug out of my hair and set in on the table, he picked it up gently and examined it. "It is trying hard to take off," he remarked. When it did, only to land on his arm, he observed, "It was hardly worth taking off for such a short flight!"

He told many stories of the desert, its beauty and its danger, mysteriously linked. Stories bloomed from his conversation like monstrous flowers, leaving us spellbound, oblivious of where we were or what we were doing. Listening to one of these while driving in the car, my meticulous husband absentmindedly ran out of gas! The desert obviously had Saint-Exupéry in thrall. But one never forgot that he was a Frenchman, rooted in France. He spoke nostalgically about Provence, the region of his old home, where he said we must go and which we would like, and of people he would like us to meet. We in turn spoke of Illiec, our wild Breton island, where we wanted him to come. "Though in this changing world," I wrote, "I fear none of these things will come true. We are living in a dream interlude—before what cataclysm I don't know but fear." We never saw him again but because of this brief interlude on the eve of hostilities, Saint-Exupéry became for me the lens through which I saw the war.

"The war," as we have been reminded lately by the anniversary celebrations of its end, is now forty years behind us. America has had two wars since. We have other problems today, many of which Saint-Exupéry foresaw: "Once the German problem has been dealt with . . . then the fundamental problem of our time will have to be considered: the meaning and purpose of humanity."

What does this writer, man of action, moralist and hero in an age of anti-heroes, have to say to us today in his last writings? Certainly, all his early admirers will want to read his observations, conflicts, and beliefs during the war itself and trace the unraveled mystery of his disappearance on his final reconnaissance mission over France.

For those to whom he is unknown or forgotten, one might glance again at his most popular little book, still read by children everywhere and, happily, by adults reading to children. What does it say? What is the secret of its popularity? Why are we universally drawn to it? The Little Prince, if you remember, comes down to earth from his miniature planet, touching several other worlds briefly en route. He is confused and distressed by what he finds on these outer realms. He meets a king who only wants to wield authority; a conceited man who lives for applause; a businessman who counts the stars; a geographer at a desk with his nose buried in scientific data; and a lamplighter, obeying outworn orders. None of these planetary beings can give him any reason for their occupations, or any sense of life. At last, on Earth's African desert, he meets a snake and a little fox who give him some answers. What is the point of life? What is essential?

"What is essential," says the little fox, "is invisible to the eye. One can only see with the heart." What is important are the bonds that link us to one another in a concept greater than oneself.

Basically this myth and its ramifications run through Saint-Exupéry's books. Myths speak to us with more immediacy than sermons. This is why we listen to *The Little Prince*. The message is there in all Saint-Exupéry's writing—more openly, perhaps, in his unfinished posthumous book, *The Wisdom of the Sands*, where a desert monarch meditates and gives advice to his subjects, again on "what is essential" and "what is invisible." But it is harder for us to accept in this form.

Wartime Writings is not another *Little Prince* but it carries again what Saint-Exupéry wanted to give to man. Collected after his death, the book is not a polished whole, nor could it possibly be. We have the impression that we are looking at the back of a beautiful tapestry. His finished books (rewritten, he claimed, as much as thirty times) are the tapestries, with the pattern standing out clearly in design and color. In this collection we see the underside, full of knots, tangles, and broken threads pieced together. Here, one realizes, is what his books cost him; what, in fact, his passion for perfection cost him in action as well as art; what his sense of nobility and dedication cost him in life and, finally, in death. The pattern, although intermittent, is still visible on the underside.

This miscellaneous collection contains letters, notes, speeches, prefaces, and a long letter (later published in book form) to a friend caught in occupied France. Here is an account of his terrible ordeal of inaction after the collapse of France. He was, he tells us, against the armistice and "stole" a transport plane in Bordeaux to convey forty young pilots to North Africa in a vain attempt to continue the war there. When he discovered that the armistice extended to North Africa as well as France, he was at an impasse. In this period, the Vichy government was being formed under the aged Marshal Pétain. Without being consulted, Saint-Exupéry found himself nominated for a position on the Vichy National Council, an offer he immediately refused. He did not, however, feel he could join the "Free French" group behind General de Gaulle. ("I should have followed him with joy against the Germans, but could not follow him against Frenchmen.") He opposed any division of France into warring camps, and foresaw the bitterness and bloodshed that would follow. With enormous difficulty he obtained a passport for the United States, hoping to persuade President Roosevelt to release American aircraft for use in Europe. In December 1940 he sailed from Lisbon to America.

Once established in New York, he was depressed by the isolationist reaction of American citizens to war and shocked by the conflicts between exiled French groups. Many friends welcomed him warmly, but gossip about his (rejected) nomination to the Vichy National Council brought insults and calumny from Gaullists. Partly to answer his critics and partly to plead for American aid, he turned to writing two more books. *Flight to Arras* describes the hazardous air missions he carried out in the early months of war. In nine months of flights over Germany his reconnaissance group lost three-quarters of its members. The swift collapse of France, he claims, was due to the criminal lack of equipment ("We set up our haystacks against their tanks"), and to the unequal strength of the forces engaged (the French were outnumbered two to one by the Germans). More profoundly, *Flight to Arras* expresses his belief in man's responsibility for man. "As the inheritor of God, my civilization made each responsible for all, and all responsible for each." "A Democracy must be a brotherhood, otherwise it is a lie."

Letter to a Hostage is his expression of deep anxiety for a friend hidden in occupied France. "The man who haunts my memory tonight is fifty years old. He is ill. He is a Jew. Will he survive the German terror?" As the letter lengthens, one realizes that Saint-Exupéry is pleading for understanding of France itself. All France was being held hostage—forty million hostages silenced by the occupation. Those Frenchmen outside of France, he argues, could not properly judge her, but only serve her. "It is always in the deepest recesses of oppression that new truths are born."

The Little Prince has overtones of farewell—perhaps to all his readers. In 1941 the "miracle" for which he had waited took place: The United States entered the war. With the recapture of North Africa, Saint-Exupéry was at last able to return to the fighting front under U.S. Army auspices. He crossed the Atlantic in a convoy with 50,000 American soldiers who "were going to war not for the citizens of the United States, but for man, for human respect. . . . How could I forget," he writes in a letter to Americans, "the great cause for which the American people fought?"

On arriving in Tunisia, Saint-Exupéry was assigned to his old Group 2/33, now based there under the Allied Photo Reconnaissance Command. Before he could carry out missions he was trained for several months in a converted P-38 Lightning, in which photographic equipment replaced guns. In July 1943 he was sent on his first photographic mission over France, flying down the Rhône Valley and above his much loved landscape of Provence. But because American regulations had set 35 as the maximum age for a P-38 pilot, Saint-Exupéry, then 43, had difficulty persuading the authorities to allow him to continue on active duty, the only assignment he desired or would accept. "I have no taste for war, but I cannot remain behind the lines." By special intervention, after an acutely depressing eight-month delay, he was finally allowed to fly five missions over France. He carried out eight and never returned from the ninth mission.

What Saint-Exupéry wrote between 1939 and 1944 was not addressed just to immediate issues, urgent as those were to him. These pages are illumined with searchlight beams into the future. The warning phrases ring in the mind with prophetic clarity. "Somewhere along the way we have gone astray. The human anthill is richer than ever before. We have more wealth and more leisure, and yet we lack something essential. . . . We feel less human; somewhere we have lost our mysterious prerogatives."

He has much to say about these prerogatives, which the war and his forced exile had clarified for him. "What frightens me more than the war is the world of tomorrow. . . . I don't mind death, but I do mind the spiritual community being endangered." Like many artists and writers of our century, he viewed the technological civilization of the West with apprehension, but not without hope. In his letter of gratitude and advice to Americans he elaborates on this theme: "You see it seems that something new is emerging on our planet. It is true that technical progress in modern times has linked men together like a complex nervous system. The means of travel are numerous and communication is instantaneous—we are joined together like the cells of a single body, but this body has as yet no soul."

And surely we are now ready to hear his plea for peace, born out of his hatred of war, written before the atom bomb fell on Hiroshima, and long before its deadly power had expanded worldwide and grown to its present towering threat.

"Let there be an end to games that have become too dangerous to be played, that destroy more than they save. . . ! If we do not all want to die in the mud, we must make peace someday. . . . There are so many conquests open to man!"

—Anne Morrow Lindbergh

Germany. I once asked Lazareff what impression Hitler had made on Chamberlain, who had just been in contact with him.

"Tremendous," he answered.

It was to be expected. If you confronted Bergson with Attila, Attila would undoubtedly astound Bergson. As for Bergson, he could not possibly make any impression on Attila.

A drunken sailor makes more noise than a philosopher. And the SS man who, thumbs stuck in his belt, walks up and down beside a humiliated physicist as he bends over to clean the latrines likewise astounds the physicist.

Saint-Exupéry[1]

In order to cure a feeling of malaise, you have to throw light on it. And we certainly live in a condition of malaise. We have chosen to save peace. But in saving peace we have harmed our friends. And no doubt many among us were ready to risk their lives in the interests of friendship and now feel a kind of shame. But if they had sacrificed peace, they would feel the same shame; because they would then have sacrificed humanity: They would have accepted the irretrievable destruction of the libraries, cathedrals, and laboratories of Europe. They would have accepted the ruin of its traditions and transformed the world into a cloud of ashes. And that is why we shifted from one opinion to the other. When peace seemed threatened, we discovered the shame of war. When it appeared that we were to be spared from war, we felt the shame of peace.

· · ·

And if the Germans are ready today to shed their blood for Hitler, you must understand that it is useless to blame Hitler. It is because Hitler gives the Germans something to be enthusiastic about and offer up their lives for that, for those Germans, Hitler is great. Don't you understand that the power of a movement depends on the human beings it produces?

Don't you understand that self-sacrifice, willingness to take risks, and faithfulness unto death are the qualities upon which the greatness of human beings is based? When you look for an example to illustrate this, you find it in the pilot who sacrifices himself for the mail he carries, in the doctor who dies combatting an epidemic, or in the officer who goes forward, at the head of his camel corps, into a desert of want and loneliness. Each year, some die. Even if their sacrifice seems pointless, do you think they have not served a purpose? They have, first of all, imprinted in the virgin human clay a beautiful image; they have sown even the heart of the little child rocked to sleep with tales born of their deeds. Nothing is lost; even the monastery surrounded by walls sheds its light.

Don't you understand that somewhere along the way we have gone astray? The human anthill is richer than ever before. We have more wealth and more leisure, and yet we lack something essential, which we find it difficult to describe. We feel less human; somewhere we have lost our mysterious prerogatives.

. . .

What then are the expanses that we wish opened up for us? We are seeking to free ourselves from the prison walls that close in about us. It was thought that in order for us to grow it was enough to dress and feed us and to pander to all our wants. Thus, bit by bit, we became the petit bourgeois of Courteline,*

---

* Georges Moinaux (called Courteline, 1858–1929) wrote bitter satirical comedies for the stage.

the village politician, the technician without any inner life. "We have been taught," you will reply, "we have been enlightened, we have been enriched more than anyone before us by the conquests of reason." But he who thinks that the culture of the mind is based on the knowledge of a series of formulae or the memorizing of acquired knowledge has a very poor idea of culture. Even the most mediocre Polytechnique student knows more about nature and law than Descartes, Pascal, or Newton. He is nevertheless incapable of a single one of the thought processes that Descartes, Pascal, or Newton were capable of. These were cultivated men first and foremost. Pascal is primarily a style, Newton a man—he mirrors the universe. The ripe apple that fell in a meadow, the stars on a night in July, spoke to him in a language he could understand. Science for him was life.

And now we find, to our surprise, that there are mysterious conditions that fertilize us. We breathe only if we are bound to others by a common aim outside ourselves. We, sons of plenty, find an inexplicable comfort in sharing out our last rations in the desert. Among those of us who have known the great joy of breakdowns and repairs in the Sahara, all other pleasures seem futile.

Therefore do not be surprised. He who never suspected the unknown dormant within him, but felt it stir just once, in an anarchist meeting in Barcelona—because of the sacrifice of life, because of mutual aid and a rigorous image of justice—will never recognize any other truth but the truth of anarchy. And he who once stood guard to protect a community of terrified little nuns in a Spanish convent will die for the Church of Spain.

. . .

There are two million men in Europe without aim or direction who ought to be reborn. Industry has torn them up from their ancestral peasant roots and confined them in those vast ghettos that resemble a giant marshaling yard cluttered with lines of black cars. Out of the depths of these dormitory towns they ought to be reborn.

There are others caught in the mesh of various jobs, to whom the joys of a Mermoz,* or of the religious life, or of the scientist, are unknown, and who also wish to be reborn.

One can, of course, endow them with life by putting them into uniform. Then they will sing songs of war and share their bread with their comrades. They will have found what they were seeking, a taste of the universal. But they will die from eating the bread they are given.

One can dig up the wooden idols and revive the old slogans, which have more or less proved their appeal in the past; one can revive the pan-German myths or those of the Roman Empire. One can make the Germans drunk with the ecstasy of being German and of being compatriots of Beethoven. One can cram them with such provender. That is certainly easier than producing another Beethoven.

But these demagogic idols are carnivorous. Someone who dies for the progress of knowledge or the curing of disease serves life's purpose even in dying. It is sweet to die for the expansion of Germany, Italy, or Japan, but then the enemy is no longer the equation that defies integration or the cancer that defies the serum—the enemy is the man next door. One has to fight him, but there is no longer any question of defeating him. Each retires behind a cement wall. Each, for better or for worse, orders nightly attacks that hit the enemy in the gut. Victory goes to the one who rots last—look at Spain—and both adversaries rot together.

What did we need in order to be reborn? To *give* ourselves. We dimly apprehended that one human being cannot communicate with another except through the same imagery. Pilots meet in the fight for the mailbag—just like the followers of

---

* Jean Mermoz (1901–36), French aviator, disappeared on a flying mission.

Hitler if they sacrifice themselves for him, or like mountain climbers if they strain toward the same summit. Men are drawn together not by confronting each other but only by sharing similar ideals. We were thirsting for comradeship in a world that had become a desert. The taste of bread shared among comrades made us accept the values of war. But when straining toward the same goal, we do not need war in order to feel the warmth of companionship. War deceives us. Hate adds nothing to the exaltation of the contest.

Saint-Exupéry wrote these words at the beginning of October 1938,[2] just after the Munich Agreement, in which the democracies of the West allowed Hitler to annex the Sudetenland in hopes of avoiding war.

Saint-Exupéry had ample time to meditate on war, ever since reporting from Spain for Paris-Soir *in June 1937.[3] Hostilities in Spain ceased on March 28, but (he noted in his diary) the world political situation made a general war foreseeable—a war that was "intellectually" unacceptable, but coming all the same.*

In February 1939, before taking a trip to Germany, Saint-Exupéry published Wind, Sand and Stars. *One line of his thinking at the time—which recurred when he joined up again for active service in more sophisticated aircraft in 1943—involved the relationship between the pilot and his machine and between sensibility and calculation. On August 1, 1939 an issue of the journal* Document *—concerning test pilots—was published under the editorship of Jean-Marie Conty, for which Saint-Exupéry wrote the following preface:*

Jean-Marie Conty will speak to you here of test pilots. Conty is a graduate of the Ecole Polytechnique and believes in equations. He is right to do so. Equations codify experience. It is rare in practice, however, that a device derives from mathematical analysis as the chick bursts out of the egg. Mathematical analysis sometimes precedes experience, but often merely codifies it—which is nevertheless an essential function. Rough measurements show that the variations of a given phenomenon are perfectly represented by a hyperbolic curve. The theoretician codifies these experimental measurements in an equation corresponding to the hyperbolic curve; but he also shows, in lengthy analyses, that it could not have been otherwise. When more precise measurements have made it possible for him to more accurately draw his graph (which now looks far more like the graph of a completely different formula), he will codify the phenomenon with infinite precision, using a new equation. He will then prove, by more painstaking analysis, that this was foreseeable from the start.

The theoretician believes in logic and believes that he despises dreams, intuition, and poetry. He does not recognize that these three fairies have only disguised themselves in order to dazzle him like a love-sick fifteen-year-old. He does not know that he owes his greatest discoveries to them. They introduced themselves in the guise of "working hypotheses," "arbitrary conditions," and "analogies"; how could he, the theoretician, have guessed that he was deceiving austere logic, and that in listening to them he was listening to the Muses' song. . . .

Jean-Marie Conty will tell you of the splendid existence of the test pilots. But he is a product of the Polytechnique. And he will tell you that soon the test pilot will be no more than a measuring instrument for the engineer. And I, like him, believe this. I also believe that the day will come when, if we feel ill without knowing why, we will go to a physicist, who without asking us anything will draw blood into a syringe, derive certain data, multiply these, and then, having consulted a table of logarithms, cure us with a pill. For the moment, nevertheless, if I fell sick I would still go to an old country doctor, who would look me up and down, pat my stomach, put a handkerchief over my chest and listen awhile, then cough, fill his pipe, and, stroking his chin, smile at me in order to cure me.

I still believe in Coupet, Lasne, or Détroyat, for whom an airplane is not merely a collection of parameters, but an organism that you examine. They land; they discreetly take a look around the plane. With the tips of their fingers they touch the fuselage and pat the wing. They do not calculate, they meditate. Then they turn to the engineer and simply say: "The fixed surface must be shortened."

I admire science, but I also admire wisdom.

de Saint-Exupéry

Saint-Exupéry, asked to write a preface for the French edition of Anne Morrow Lindbergh's Listen! The Wind, *cabled after reading the proofs (July 10, 1939):*

OVERWHELMED BY THE LINDBERGH PROOFS. WOULD WISH TO WRITE IMPORTANT INSTEAD OF SHORT PREFACE IF TEXT DELIVERY JULY 15 ON RETURN NEW YORK NOT TOO LATE FOR YOU.

Preface to the French edition of *Listen! The Wind* (extracts)[4]

. . . The real book is like a net whose words make up the mesh. The important factor is the living prey that the fisherman has dragged out of the deep, those shafts of silver that glint through the mesh. What has Anne Lindbergh brought forth from her inner life? What texture does her book have?

It is difficult to define. In order to explain it, one would have to write a book and speak of many things. Nevertheless, I feel there is, running through these pages, a very slight anxiety which takes different forms but flows continuously like a silent bloodstream. . . .

What Anne Lindbergh has expressed—to put it in a nut-shell—is the bad conscience one feels in having a taste for being late. How difficult it is to advance at one's own internal rhythm, when one is constantly fighting against the inertia of the material world. Everything is always on the verge of stopping. How vigilant one has to be to preserve life and movement in a world on the verge of breaking down. . . .

Lindbergh is steering a little boat in the bay of Porto-Praïa in order to make a survey. She sees him from the top of a hill, like a tiny insect exhausting itself when caught in a sticky mass. Every time she turns toward the sea on her walk, it seems to her that her husband has not moved. The insect moves its wing-sheaths in vain. How difficult it is to cross a bay. Even slowing down slightly would mean never reaching the other side at all.

For days the two of them have been prisoners on an island where time has no meaning, where time does not flow, where men live and die having no more than one small thought in their brains, always the same one, which one day stops.

(Their host gabbles over and over again, "I'm the boss here . . . ," with the indifference of a far-off echo.) Time must be got moving again. They must go back to the continent, re-join the mainstream, where one is worn down, where one lives. Anne Lindbergh is afraid not of death but of eternity.

Eternity is so close! It takes so little never to cross a bay, never to leave an island, never to take off from Bathurst. They are both a little late, Lindbergh and she . . . so very little . . . barely. . . . But one only needs to be a little too late and no one in the world expects one any longer.

We have known the little girl who runs less fast than the others. Over there, the others are playing. "Wait for me! Wait for me!" But she is a little too late. They will get tired of waiting; she will be left behind; she will be forgotten, alone in the world. How could one reassure her? This form of anxiety is incurable. For if she now takes part in the games but will have to leave and puts off leaving, she will weary her friends! Already they are murmuring among themselves, already they are looking askance at her. . . . They will once again leave her alone in the world!

And this secret anxiety is an extraordinary revelation on the part of this couple, acclaimed the world over. A cable from Bathurst tells them they are invited there, and they are infinitely grateful. Later, they are unable to take off from Bathurst and feel ashamed at foisting themselves on the organizers. There is no question of false modesty here, but of the feeling of mortal danger. A little too late and all is lost.

Fruitful anxiety. It is this inner remorse that forces them to make a start two hours before dawn, to precede even the front-runners, to cross the stormy oceans that still impede the others.

How far removed we are from those stories that string together events with the arbitrariness of hunting tales! How well Anne Lindbergh secretly underpins her tale with something that defies definition, something as elemental and universal as a myth. How well Anne Lindbergh conveys the central problem of the human condition in recounting technical jottings and concrete problems. She does not write about the plane but through her experience of the plane. This stock of professional images is used as a vehicle to convey to us something confidential but essential.

Lindbergh has not taken off from Bathurst. The plane is too heavily laden. It would only take a sea breeze for the plane to lift off, but there is none. And the two of them once again fight against the quagmire. Then they decide to sacrifice stores, accessories, and the less essential spare parts. They renew their takeoff attempts—which fail. And each time they lighten the plane's load. And little by little their lodging is littered with the precious items they have unloaded, adding ounce upon ounce with infinite regret. . . .

Anne Lindbergh conveys this minor professional heartbreak with piercing clarity. And she does not misrepresent the pathetic nature of the plane. This pathos is not just made up of pink evening clouds, like a sort of stage set. It can concern the use of a screwdriver when you leave a black hole—like a broken tooth—in the symmetry of the instrument panel. But make no mistake: If the author succeeds in making the layman as well as the professional pilot feel this melancholy, it is because she has conveyed—beyond this purely professional pathos—the general pathos of humanity. She has rediscovered the old myth of the sacrifice that sets free. We already know those trees that have to be pruned in order to bear fruit and those men who, in their monastery prisons, discover their spiritual range and by progressive renunciation gain spiritual plenitude. . . .

But the help of the gods is also necessary and Anne Lindbergh rediscovers Fatality. It is not enough to cut into a man's heart in order to save him—he must be touched by grace. It is not enough to prune a tree in order to make it bear fruit—spring must come, too. It is not enough to lighten the plane's cargo—there must be a sea breeze as well.

Without trying to, Anne Lindbergh has renewed the myth of Iphigenia. She writes at a high enough level for her fight against time to become a fight against death, in order for the lack of wind at Bathurst to become for us a question of destiny. She makes us perceive how the seaplane, which on the water is only a heavy and unwieldy machine, changes its nature and becomes a highly sensitive thoroughbred as soon as the sea breeze touches it.

Saint-Exupéry went to America at the request of his American publishers. He told a journalist that he had just discovered Anne Morrow Lindbergh's talent: "I feared a potboiler and I thought that in a few brief lines I should be able to present the translation to French readers. . . . But not at all! As I read further, I was gripped, and started asking myself all sorts of questions." For Saint-Exupéry, it was "a very human book. . . . Anne Lindbergh does not write about the plane, but as though the plane were part of her." And the well-known theme recurs: "Mrs. Lindbergh and he believe that there will always be something more admirable than a running engine: namely a heart that beats. They do not allow themselves to be bowled over by the machine."

Saint-Exupéry sailed for France again in August, arriving in Le Havre on the 30th. A few days earlier the Hitler-Stalin Pact had been signed. Hitler invaded Poland on September 1. Two days later France and England declared war on Germany.

In the first week of September Saint-Exupéry was mobilized and assigned to the airbase at Toulouse-Moutaudran, where he occupied the post of instructor of aerial navigation.

Jean Giraudoux, High Commissioner for Information, would have liked to see him join the propaganda service. The following text was a radio broadcast, probably recorded on October 16.

The Propaganda of Pan-Germanism[5]
(Message broadcast October 18, 1939)

German propaganda has worked brilliantly, like those teams that produce special effects for Hollywood films.

The German propaganda teams were faced each time with the following problem: Germany, in order to expand, must absorb a given territory. How could they present this new demand to the world in such a way as to disturb its common sense and confuse its conscience? So the teams launched slogans. The slogans contradicted each other, but, as advertising agencies know, crowds have no memory.

For a long time we were fooled. We seriously discussed the justification of their motives; we tried not to denigrate the adversary's line of argument, but to appeal to his good faith and make him ashamed of his contradictions. We used words where words were not appropriate.

All those formulas were only posters, the purpose of which

was to give Germany more lands to swallow, whatever the race, population density, or spiritual needs of the populations of those new lands.

We became entangled in the mere rules and regulations that our adversaries offered us, and we had some excuse for this. We were human beings and thought that human beings were inspired in their behavior by philosophies, religions, or doctrines. We believed that if human beings were ready to fight and die for a cause, it must be because this cause appealed to their idealism. We had forgotten that some motives for action have nothing to do with idealism and that a country may tend to expand as any blind organism does.

We had forgotten this, because for us civilization represented the conquest of mind over elementary urges. But over there, the mind was only a lackey charged with justifying the urges of the organism. Crusading pan-Germanism relies on Goethe or Bach. And thus Goethe or Bach, whom Germany today would leave to rot in a concentration camp or expel like Einstein, are used to justify mustard gas and the bombardment of open cities. But pan-Germanism has nothing to do with Goethe or Bach harnessed to its purposes. It has nothing to do with the ideology of peoples' rights, nothing to do with necessary *Lebensraum*. It is merely a question of space for its own sake. Pan-Germanism is the tendency toward expansion. It is a tendency found in all animal species. Every race tends to multiply and exterminate the others.

If there is any justification for pan-Germanism, it is this— and this is not merely a witticism; we will encounter it in a veiled way in all Nazi writings. The argument runs: We Germans deserve to expand, to absorb our neighbors and use their goods for our aggrandizement, because a desire for expansion is a sign of vigor and we are the only ones who feel this appetite. Our superiority over our adversaries is contained in our wish to absorb them, whereas our degenerate adversaries are incapable of such a desire.

And so we know now that laying down our arms would mean confirming Germany's appetite. The monstrous Nazi-Soviet Pact has forever sealed off the route of expansion eastward. Who will feed their appetite tomorrow? Germany cannot be explained by means of reasoned ideologies. She does not follow definable goals. Germany's goals are nothing but a succession of tactical advances, of publicity stunts. The real aim of Germany is to expand.

That is why for us today it is not merely a question of fighting against Nazism, or for Poland, or for the Czechs, or for our civilization, but to fight in order to survive. Those who have left their farms, their shops, their factories, fight in order not to become mere fertilizer for German prosperity. They have gone out to gain the right to live and to live in peace.

Saint-Exupéry was to recall the High Commissioner's invitation when he came to write Chapter V of Flight to Arras:

To be tempted is to be tempted, when the spirit is asleep, to give in to the reasons of the mind.

What do I accomplish by risking my life in this mountain avalanche? I have no notion. Time and again people would say to me, "I can arrange to have you transferred here or there. That is where you belong. You will be more useful there than in a squadron. Pilots! We can train pilots by the thousand! Whereas you——." No question but that they were right. My mind agreed with them, but my instinct always prevailed over my mind.

Why was it that their reasoning never convinced me, even though I had no argument with which to defeat it? I would say to myself, "Intellectuals are kept in reserve on the shelves of the

Propaganda Ministry, like pots of jam to be eaten when the war is over." Hardly an argument, I agree!

And now once again, like every other airman of the group, I have taken off in the face of every good reason, every obvious argument, every intellectual reflex. The moment will come when I shall know that it was reasonable to fight against reason.

Letter to X[6]

[Toulouse, October 26, 1939]

I beg you most earnestly to bring your influence to bear on Champsaur in favor of a fighter squadron. I'm feeling more and more stifled. The atmosphere here is unbearable. God Almighty, what are we waiting for?

Don't see Daurat* until you've used every means to get me into a fighter squadron. While I'm not fighting, I'm very sick, morally. I have a great deal to say about events, but I can only say it as a fighter, not as a tourist. It is my only chance of speaking. I fly four times a day, I'm in fine fettle, perhaps too much so, as things have got worse. They want to make me into a navigation instructor as well as a flying instructor for heavy bombers. I'm therefore stifling, miserable, and can only keep silent. . . . Get me into a fighter squadron. . . . I have no taste for war, but I cannot remain behind the lines and not take my share of risks. . . . We must make war. But I have no right to say so while I stroll about Toulouse in perfect safety. That is an ignoble role. Give me the right by letting me undergo the tests to which I'm entitled. There is something intellectually disgusting about pretending that one has to shelter "those who are valuable."

It is by participating that one plays an efficient part. Men

* Didier Daurat, fighter pilot 1914–18, later Saint-Exupéry's superior and mentor at Aéropostale (now Air France).

worthy of respect, if they are the salt of the earth, must then mingle with the earth. One cannot say "we" if one stands apart. To say "we" under such circumstances is to be a scoundrel.

Letter to X[7]

[Toulouse, Grand Hotel Tivollier,
early November 1939]

I have just been on guard duty for two days. I slept at the airfield among the telephones and the coded messages, woke up in a whitewashed cell and dined in a freezing mess hall, like a child in a dining hall. There I found an inexpressible joy in the noises of the building, in the routine, and in the comings and goings of the personnel. I would like to be plunged into it, right to the marrow of my bones. I feel of no significance. In this little bourgeois existence, with the dreadful Lafayette,* with these circlings of the airfield, these perambulations backward and forward in front of the hangars, I am worth nothing. I would like to be incorporated into a tree. Then I could feel all the birds I was protecting.

The bliss of anonymity, whether as an airline pilot, or a fighter pilot, or in the cloister, is that you softly and simply become something significant. One becomes transformed into something else through a sort of natural digestion.

For me, asking is not embarrassing. It is not a post or a subsidy I am asking for, but my dispatch to the front—to a fighting unit. This service is vital to me. And even if this should be difficult to accomplish, I do not hesitate to ask it of you, even if it involves complications, because it is the first time that I am asking such an important favor of you. Don't see Daurat first. Daurat won't save me. I must play my part in this religious war. Everything that I love is threatened. In Provence, when there

* A local café patronized by Saint-Exupéry and his fellow pilots.

is a forest fire, everyone who is not a dirty dog picks up a bucket and a pick. I want to fight for love and an inner religion. I just cannot *not* join up. Get me into a fighting unit as quickly as possible.

Here I am rotting in wretched uselessness. I have no illusions about my stamina as a fighter pilot, but at least I can become a kind of humus, with the same joy I felt as an airline pilot. Among the airline pilots I become a little of the earth that feeds the tree. I no longer need to understand. The purpose of the earth, then, is the tree. That much seems self-evident.

As the doctors refused to allow him to be drafted into a fighter squadron because of his age and the remaining after-effects of his flying accidents, a compromise was reached: Thanks to Colonel de Vitrolles, Saint-Exupéry was assigned (on December 3, 1939) to General Reconnaissance Group 2/33 based at Orconte (Aisne). (He did not want to fly a bomber.)

On November 26 he had begun training as a military pilot. After declining an invitation to billet himself in the local country house, Saint-Exupéry moved into a little farmhouse at Orconte.

Letter to X[8]

[Orconte, mid-December]

Mud. Rain. Rheumatism in a farmhouse. Empty evenings. The melancholy of doubt. Anxiety at 35,000 feet. Fear also, of course. Everything that is demanded of a man in order to be a man among men. And I'm united with my fellow men, because if I separate myself from them, I'm nothing. How I despise spectators. . . .

I found what I was meant to find. I'm like the others. I feel cold like the others. I've got rheumatism like the others. I had no more choice than the others. They had the gendarmes to make them join up. I had something more imperative than a gendarme behind me. Then also, I enjoy the drinking songs. But they do, too. Nevertheless, they go on leave to warm up and be consoled, cheered up, and slapped on the shoulder in a friendly way. I should like to be a completely anonymous serviceman.

Letter to X[9]

[Orconte, December 22 or 23, 1939]
Melancholy day. My group and our twin group each lost a crew shot down the same day. . . .

I loved my crash landing in Libya* and the necessity that forced me to walk and the desert that was swallowing me bit by bit. I was changing into something else, something that wasn't too bad. . . . At night I felt lost in the sands and I loved that wide navigation among the stars. Wasn't it my duty? I'm ready to believe that what we call duty is what renders the greatest service, but this is no longer so when we are speaking of contemplative truths. And contemplation is greater than charity. It is on a higher level. . . . But it has a sickening taste. One seems to be trying to set oneself off to advantage. Nobody asks anything of me, and if I were given a mission, it would not be in order to exploit me but to favor me ahead of a hundred other candidates.

Have you seen that herd of ambassadors seeking advancement? I'm not of that tribe. There, there is no imperious tree, forcibly tearing out earth's treasures and marvelously exhausting it.

* On January 2, 1936, Saint-Exupéry set out to establish a record on the Paris–Saigon run. His plane crashed in the Sahara. He and his mechanic, Jean Prévost, were picked up and saved by Bedouins.[10]

Letter to X[11]

Orconte [December 1939]

... I'm advised to take my leave now, immediately, because there will be little work during the next two weeks and much thereafter.

Don't believe my other letter. Everything is so difficult to explain and so contradictory. I'm not sorry at having made the choice, because I find life very difficult to understand and my own self too complex for me to understand. I don't know how to make use of myself. The difficult moments are those spent chasing phantasms one after another. Earlier, I didn't relish the idea of going up to 35,000 feet or of fighting. I feel no thirst for battle and I don't clearly see my own generation's role. It's more a question of accepting the 35,000 feet, the mud, and the risk of death. Only unadulterated bitterness remains, since here there is no joy of creation, of conquest, or of the hunt. I cannot bear not to take part. Thus, when you progressively tear off the layers of bark enfolding you, it pulls and hurts. But at the same time you realize that these layers are merely bark, since once you have vanquished the phantasm you couldn't care less about the 35,000 feet. It is always in the midst, in the epicenter, of your troubles that you find serenity. You have to tear off the bark....

Letter to X[12]

[Orconte, late December]
Midnight

There was a celebration at Vitry. I had to go to the armed forces' theater.* And again, more urgently than ever, I ask myself

---

* To combat boredom during the "phony war" a service for "reading, arts, and leisure activities in the forces" was set up, along with a "theater for the armed forces." Jean Dutourd says in his book *Les Taxis de la Marne* that it was the only thing that worked satisfactorily. This celebration took place on December 14.

the question, What are we fighting for? Where are the French in all this? Where is Pascal? The baseness of all this buffoonery! The baseness of these ready-made ditties! They are only bearable when they are as stupid as "Olga":

Instead of joining the services, she followed the forces.

But these turn into a pornography of the heart when they extend to feelings, when they try to stir up emotion. This is the dog food that the manufacturers give to men, who are content with it. Milton* was applauded. The sinister jollity of such a miserable clown, tormented by his piles and thinking of nothing else, but who more or less earns his keep by juggling with words—one could hardly call them phrases because phrases are structures representing inner emotions.

So, once again, I hark back to the freshness, truthfulness, and health of listening to "Olga":

As she was only half a virgin, she paid for only half her keep.

Suddenly the style emulates the content, the content being the pleasure of voicing a piece of nonsense, making a joke, or something natural like belching. The content is meager but it is carried along by the style, such as it is, without discarding or adding anything to it. But how can one stand something like:

I l-o-o-o-v-e you to d-i-str-a-a-a-ction

without vomiting?

What inner emotion was responsible for this style? I saw the author, a money-grubbing horse-trader. Even though the

* French entertainer who appeared in the armed forces theater presentation that Saint-Exupéry attended on December 14.

words are logically put together, they are nothing but the er-
uctations of a drunkard, the intestinal rumblings of the mind.
Nothing is joined together from the inside. How tasteless all
this is! Love here is nothing but the frayed purple of a ham
actor.

For a second I was touched:

When the maids go off to the woods, the priest is happy,
There will be more christenings. . . .

Suddenly I thought of towns and villages, giving them a
meaning. Giraudoux* and the present state of affairs are the
town, but a town in which everything has lost its meaning
through mental tergiversations, like my horse-trader, whose
meaning has been lost through baseness. The village carries the
idea of durability, of consanguinity, of the passage of time and
the transformations it brings. One sows corn and it grows. (If
the young girls go to the woods, the priest is pleased because of
the christenings that will follow.)

Thus, slowly, folk songs, dances, and beautiful pieces of
furniture are born. In the medieval village, where the passage
of time had a meaning, where man was part of a line—and
where words had a presence because of the Church—the dead
ensured continuity. But our dead are empty cases. And our
summer has nothing to do with autumn; they are merely jux-
taposed seasons. The disabled men of today! And Giraudoux
believes that man can be saved by his intelligence. But the intelligence that dismantles and juxtaposes the pieces (when it
doesn't actually falsify the arrangement for fun to achieve quaint-

---

* From July 1939 the playwright Jean Giraudoux was General Commissioner for
Information to the Prime Minister: He was in charge of censorship and propaganda.
His subtle and measured phrases—at a time when the whole country should have been
aroused—would later be held against him.

ness) loses the feeling for the essential. When one analyzes "situations" one no longer perceives anything human.

I'm neither young nor old. I'm midway between the two. I'm something being formed. I'm an aging process—a rose that has nothing sprouting forth, but just opens and blows. That is a pedagogical explanation, an analysis that kills the rose. A rose isn't a succession of stages. A rose is a faintly melancholy celebration.

I know exactly what I mean, but I will have to think in order to make myself clear.

About the armed forces theater: In this war . . . I'm ready to die "to fertilize the soil," but not to save Milton. I'm unhappy on account of this odd planet I live on. Because of all that I cannot understand, I'm weary, but with a weariness that is very hard to express. I probably owe this partly to J. Nothing is more painful than to see my friends lose their value in my eyes. In fact I learned nothing about J. that I didn't already know. But he bored me; I was bored in his presence. I said to myself: "I don't give a damn, I'm not interested!" I'm not interested in what he thinks about life. I'm not interested in drinking. A glass among friends for good measure—but not like that, as a ritual. And I don't care what happens to the things in his hands. He heard some beautiful tales, but they turned ugly . . . that's all. I've returned from 35,000 feet. Another ghost laid to rest. That territory at 35,000 feet, that uninhabitable land roamed by unknown animals, whence the concave earth is black and where a man's gestures become slow, like those of someone swimming in syrup—where the reduction in pressure (only one-tenth that at sea level) may make your life evaporate; where you breathe ice, since your breath at minus 51° centigrade transforms itself into thin needles along the surfaces inside the mask; where you are threatened by twenty-five different kinds of breakdowns, including failure of the inhalator, which cuts you straight off, and failure of the heating system, which literally turns you to ice. All that is true; but that is something very different. Those are only phantoms.

Of course there is the gauge on the instrument panel that controls the oxygen flow and the little needle, more important than the one that checks the heartbeat. But nevertheless that is something different, and the needle remains abstract—one doesn't see it.

One only squeezes a little rubber tube leading to the mask from time to time with the tips of one's fingers, to check that it is full. If there is milk in the baby bottle, one sucks on contentedly. There is nothing pathetic here.

As far as the possibility of the heating system breaking down was concerned, I was quite at ease up there. What filled me with amazement was that the heat was so diffuse, so beautifully spread out. I was afraid the wires would burn my skin—but not at all. No burning sensation along the wires at all. And I said to myself: "All the same, if the Eskimos had this . . . !" A masterpiece of engineering, this tepid bath—all over, except for the fingers. I had cold fingers, but it was bearable. And I flew for a long time in the sky with my hand on the trigger for the machine guns.

Then when I landed:

"What was the temperature?"

"Minus 51."

"You can't have been very warm."

"No, I was cold, but not disagreeably so. You told me that warm oxygen burns the nose, but my nose was fine. As for the boots—"

"—the boots weren't going to burn you. . . . You forgot to connect them."

And to think that before this first flight, I imagined myself fighting a slow battle against faintness. The horrible damp skin on the forehead and hands, and the sweetish feeling, a sort of perversion of the senses.

No, 35,000 feet with oxygen is easier than 25,000 feet without oxygen. And suddenly all my admiration crumbles—my admiration for Major Michy at Toulouse, the only airman I knew who faced high altitudes. These men who prove their heroism every day. They say little of their trials when they land. Heroes are like that. Rough men of few words. When they are questioned, they shrug their shoulders. "My boy, you can't understand!" Once again I discover the meaning of their silence. They have nothing to say. That is not where courage lies. Courage lies in their choice. And Michy is brave. Because everyone knows beforehand that there is a certain percentage of accidents at 35,000 feet and that they are fatal. And so it takes a special effort to choose such a profession. And then one has to decide on one's own to set out and lay the ghost to rest. One must store up the necessary provision of courage; that alone is meritorious. Once the ghost has been laid, this job becomes like any other. Flying at 35,000 feet or repairing chairs . . . where is the difference, once the ghost has been laid? I experienced this feeling on every night flight—the possibility of drowning at sea or dying of thirst. And Daurat didn't teach his flyers courage, but he forced them to lay the ghost. I've already related this in *Night Flight*.

I was so pleased the day before yesterday when my flying mission was canceled. What an idiot I was!

But then courage becomes something much nobler than the mere violence of a drunken sergeant—it becomes a condition of self-knowledge. Yes, of course, all dramas are of a social nature. Just one sick child makes a drama. A drama is always somebody else's. One's own case is never a drama. One soars to 35,000 feet and explodes and nothing remains. But one cannot enter into another person. Another person is a limitless expanse. And a little child who is cold is more painful than any breakdown of the heating system at 50° below zero. I've known cold and insecurity, but only the insecurity of others.

I don't know why I have this urge to burden myself with all this. I've taken on the burden of "their" 35,000 feet. That is "my war"—not that stupid toreador's feat that I was hurt at being entrusted with. Groups 1/33 and 2/33 lost eleven crews out of twenty or twenty-five. They were the only ones to work and take risks, and that occasionally makes me feel melancholy in my room. One pays dearly for this, but I don't really know what it is that one pays for dearly. At least I cannot define it. But at least there is a compensation, since I believe in it. This evening I'm deaf in one ear (not owing to the humming in my ears, which has lessened, but because of my first descent from so high up) and I'll have a compressed eardrum until tomorrow.

And once again I think of the incomprehensible contradiction. At times the body is oneself—the body that loves, that enjoys the peaceful evening by the fireside, that curls up under the blanket in order to sleep, that knows how to smile. And at other times the body separates itself from one and is reduced to an instrument made to work like a bullock in the field, whose ears may be shattered, whose skin may be grilled—just like some of my fellow flyers the day before yesterday. There are two feelings this evening, the sadness in the face of possible death and the melancholy dream of all the gardens that will then be closed. One thunderbolt from a Messerschmitt will be enough to set you on fire like a tree. It strikes out of a clear sky—then the silent, vertical dive.

The only one of the three who managed to save himself with his parachute saw nothing—only suddenly the controls exploded. Then fire, like a rumbling in the intestines. The subterranean work of fire. Being taken possession of by fire. And he gave up his home. And of course I'm not fireproof, either. Perhaps I'll have to lay a last ghost and that makes my heart contract with melancholy. One thinks of luxury, of hanging gardens, which to me represent an image of luxury. And then one thinks of the flesh, of the smell that makes the heart contract. The suit opens and the warm scent overwhelms you. But also another feeling, which I'll find within the act tomorrow. The body is only a means of small importance. There is no drama where the body is concerned. I know there is none. Sometimes I'm naked and cold.

How much I have to say about war. Not that I see much of it here. But where I am is a vantage point, and like all vantage points it is inspiring—an internal vantage point. I had to go through this, but the revelation is melancholy—not all of it, but some of it.

First of all, I'm happy because of the rather harsh conditions, the discomfort, cold, and damp, which make up for the tangible luxuries: the little round stove that burns so well, or my farmhouse bed—I sleep on a farm—where the eiderdown seems to me the very symbol of opulence. I love it at night when I lie down and roll up into a ball in my icy bed to produce my own warmth and dreams; I enjoy feeling the river of cold I encounter whenever I move a foot. I feel good once the snow has melted—and naturally my bronchitis is cured.

Then of course there are the flights. I haven't yet crossed the lines, but I've been up in the air. And since one may meet with the enemy, I was taught—before taking off—how to use the machine guns. I have no taste for sport. Perhaps there is a misunderstanding. I like whatever forces me to come out of myself. I don't like altitude; 35,000 feet is not an inhabited world, and it strongly affects me to realize that if the inhalator failed I would be strangled like a chicken.

This splitting myself into two, this distancing myself from myself—I must take no account of the tightening in the gut that can hit any one of us. Life on the surface is without interest. I'm not here. I live elsewhere. I need to be content with myself when I wake up. My fellow flyers are another problem—a problem of quality for one thing—but there are so many ways to judge. One doesn't know how to tackle the problem, having all one's life preferred those who enjoy Bach to those who enjoy the tango.

And then one fights with those who turn off good music when it comes on the air. But they have the great fundamental qualities. And then those who fight best, the only ones who really fight, don't fight for the same reasons that I do. They're not fighting to save our civilization. Or if they were, one would have to redefine civilization and what it comprises.

The vast absurdity of the present time weighs on my heart. It's always the same: The present is not thought out, because for the last hundred years everything has changed too fast and thought is a slow process.

Imagine a physicist who is given (all at once) twenty new fractions of known phenomena and a thousand new phenomena. The problem would be too much for him. One would have to wait for centuries for someone who—having slowly digested all this—could create a new language that could put the world in order. There would be no more order in mathematical physics. All this is extremely bitter. There are no longer many possible positions: either to accept being Hitler's slave—or to reject him entirely, taking on the risks inherent in this refusal. All this in silence. I don't want to speak on the radio; it is indecent when you have no bible to offer people. And I accept the inherent risks of my refusal. But I had to cross the bar in order to get the full measure of what it means to give up peace. I know what it is that I am in principle giving up—freedom, the bodily warmth of love, and perhaps life. And, I ask myself, for what? And this question is as painful as a religious doubt—and no doubt as fertile. It is the intolerable contradiction that forcibly creates the truth. Because I'm up to my neck in contradictions. Either I will die or I will come to terms with myself. But it is certainly not in *Paris-Soir* that I shall find spiritual peace. Nor with M. Ramon Fernandez,* nor on the hideous radio. I listened to Pierre Dac† yesterday—stunned. If I were a foreigner and heard France spewing out that drivel, I would consider it urgent to rid the world of such trash. *Paris-Soir* yesterday published a surprising and lengthy article on Hitler the warlord—the biggest publicity stunt Hitler could ever have dreamed up. It gives an indubitable impression of grandeur. And the censors let it through! They all act like monkeys in front of a boa constrictor. This country is lost unless it is given clear reasons for fighting. . . . Visibly, nothing inspires it. It is therefore no surprise that we follow England's lead—we're unable to define ourselves, to delineate our features. The English fight for their customs, their Ceylon tea, their weekends. We feel a vague solidarity but we have no such general or clear-cut customs.

And so England becomes M. Daladier's‡ conscience and our conscience. And we would no longer be at war if England had not made us feel ashamed. And we feel resentful toward England—as one does toward a too-exacting conscience. It is here that the inadequacy of Giraudoux and his method becomes obvious. The mental tricks of an intellectual pitted against race and unity! Those jugglings with words! No one is ready to die for a method or a cocktail recipe. All that is terribly abstract, amusing, and attractive to the mind, but it makes no impression on the heart. It's not enough for me to be ready to accept death by fire. (I've discovered that my broken shoulder will not allow me to bail out with a parachute.) So much the better, because I take my risks more seriously. And so I'll have to understand. But when my opposite number shouts "Heil Hitler!" I won't be shouting: "Long live measured words!"§

* The writer had visited Saint-Exupéry's squadron on December 16.

† A popular comedian and singer.

‡ Edouard Daladier (1884–1970), Prime Minister of France in 1933, 1934, and again from 1938 until his resignation in March 1940.

§ See the note on Giraudoux at the beginning of this letter.

Something strikes me once again—the gentlest thing on this strange mountain that I'm sitting on alone. I feel tender toward all those I love and more tender toward all mankind. It's always the same. When one is in danger one is responsible for all. One feels like saying: "Peace be with you."

1940

War must be waged . . . but, as the fundamental problem is never tackled, this war will only end with the momentary exhaustion of one of the adversaries.

Saint-Exupéry, 1940[1]

Recollections of Jean Israël[2]

Taking advantage of a beautiful starless night, the squadron leader of Group 2/33 decided that the evening of January 12, 1940 would be used to practice night landings. The pilots had to land without floodlights, with the sole aid of restricted ground lights showing a landing axis.

Saint-Exupéry was one of the pilots taking part in this training. An error of interpretation of the line of ground lights made him follow a flight path that brought him head-on into the path of a truck carrying a spare floodlight. A few feet from the ground, seeing the ground lights disappear, he realized there was a dark obstacle straight ahead of him.

To stop a plane's descent, you have to maneuver by pulling on the stick; the descent tails off and is followed by an ascent. Saint-Exupéry instead pushed the stick forward. The plane nose-dived, its wheels hitting the ground hard, and it rebounded over the obstacle, while the pilot revved the engine to gain altitude and circle the field once more.

Any other maneuver would have been pointless; the plane was too near the ground and would have crashed into the truck.

Saint-Exupéry did not have to "invent" this maneuver. He had merely applied—with incredible presence of mind—a lesson learned in his days with Aéropostale. At the time he was flying single-engine planes of delicate construction, and forced landings in the countryside were quite frequent. If the landing site chosen turned out—at the last moment—to be traversed by a ditch, you had to hit the ground hard with the wheels to bounce over the ditch.

This technique, buried in some obscure corner of his memory, is what came back to Saint-Exupéry at this critical moment.

Let no one tell me that Saint-Exupéry was not a good pilot. I was sitting in the front seat of the plane that night!

Letter to X[3]

[January 1940]

I came to Nancy by plane for a few hours. . . . I acted very foolishly in that business with the truck, but I was very tense. The fundamental cause is very difficult to explain. After certain irretrievable mistakes, one would like to retrace one's steps to the place where one took the wrong turning. One would so much like not to have said this, not to have done that. A sense of irrevocability is added to the feeling of pain. All that was fluid and changing has suddenly set into rigid lines. A past event is like a wandering stone fallen from heaven. One can neither move it nor penetrate it. It now occupies a field that was clear yesterday, and I shall have to take its presence into account. One makes a gesture one shouldn't have made—and the whole future has solidified. All that was soft clay to be sculpted has suddenly hardened. And one feels the weight of real injustice. Injustice is the irrevocable. Injustice is the impossibility of redemption (no doubt this is the only injustice). Injustice is first and foremost an enormous intangible stone, formed at the expense of living things that one could influence once and to which one could return. Injustice is the gouging out of the eyes.

The sight of the black truck thirty feet from me as I sped toward it at 110 miles an hour. And I "should have" pulled the stick back in order to clear it. . . . I had not a hundredth of a second to think it over. The surest reflex had to come into play. I could not go back to the beginning of events and begin again at the crucial parting of the ways. Certainly I chose the right solution, but I saw the other, saw it at such close quarters and so much more likely than the right one. Out of a hundred chances against one, that solution was open to me.

. . . I'm not afraid of death. I'm afraid of what will be past. I was not afraid of the black truck appearing out of the night like a monster, but of the mess. And when I circled the field again in the darkness, I barely thought of missing the landing strip, of the possibility of catching fire, of all those trifles. I carried in my mind's eye a much weightier image. For you, the plane was visible, since it was vaguely lit up. But for me, dazzled by the lights, all the rest was darkness. When I chose to hit the ground in order to bounce over it, I had the impression of burrowing into the earth up to my midriff before leaping over. I left a dip in the ground behind me, like a nest molded in my shape. But I didn't know what I had hatched in that nest. I didn't know what I should find in the rounded mold of my chest. And since those idiots took their time before switching on the floodlights again, I thought: There it is. . . . I've killed them all.

Then, after landing, when I found out that you of all people were there . . . I was in a rather depressed mood in the car. And I wasn't very eager to go back, really—which is understandable.

The next day, driving toward La Ferté, I felt I was driving along one of the two roads that forked at the exact moment when—without reason or the intervention of my brain and against all my reflexes—I had chosen to crash into the ground. I was driving toward La Ferté, but the other me, which had chosen the other gesture, the more likely one, was also driving along the other road. And this other me, biting his fingertips horribly, was saying to himself: If only I could make that gesture of a tenth of a second over again! If I could only go back in time and choose to bang myself down. . . . Then, instead of living through this ghastly nightmare, I'd be happily driving in the sunshine on the road to La Ferté. . . .

Then I was irritated by the jamming noise, by the badly adjusted headlights, by all the inertia of the material world. The other—so negligent in adjusting my headlights: "I'm late . . . I've had your headlights fixed." He seemed to me like those who set up the landing axis, with the two first lights leading right toward the obstacles. And I was indignant. The negligence in checking the aircraft. "You may take off, as is." It was like saying, "Take off, it may function once you're airborne. . . ." But the intercom, the machine guns, the radio all break down. It is too late to deal with them, and one slides irremediably into the shadows. And I was still indignant.

On January 16, Group 2/33 moved to Athiès-sous-Laon. On January 19, the field-mess was installed in the little village of Monceau-le-Vast, near Laon. Saint-Exupéry had not yet flown on a single military mission.

After a first visit to La Ferté-sous-Jarre, to the general headquarters where he met the Air Force Commander, General Vuillemin, Saint-Exupéry had to go to the Air Ministry in Paris, in order to obtain permission to remain with Group 2/33. Several of his friends, including Daurat, took part in this "conspiracy" to shelter him against his own wishes.

Letter to X[4]

[Orconte, mid-January 1940]

We move today or tomorrow because of the combined German-Belgian menace. I'm saddened at shifting my quarters. I'd got used to my little farmhouse, the village streets, and the barracks on the airstrip.

As soon as the snow permits, we'll take off. It is snowing. I went to see General Têtu. He asked me to dinner. I explained everything and he understood it all. However, things depend not on Vuillemin but on Gamelin. . . .*

It is not enough to be right. It is not reasons that sway decisions. But when it's a question of Gamelin, Vuillemin, Guy La Chambre,† and Daladier, you say they understand and make decisions "because you are right" and you imagine philosophical epistles about this. They don't care a damn. There is only one course of action: human contact, words, anger, warmth. . . .

We're moving on, but the address remains the same. . . .

Letter to X[5]

[January 27, 1940]
Hôtel de Laon

I'm so disgusted with my new life. This central heating, this mirror wardrobe, this semi-luxury, this middle-class life. Only now, little by little, do I discover how much I liked Orconte; how much my farm-life, my icy room, the mud and snow made me feel part of myself. And then there were the 35,000 feet to make one feel serious.

Once again I'm at a loss—I can't gather myself together. My promises were kept over there. I was just beginning to thaw,

---

* Maurice Gamelin (1872–1958), Commander in Chief of French forces from June 1939 to May 1940.
† Air Force Minister.

slowly, very slowly. What can I do with this useless machine?

I didn't want this routine life. I wanted to join the others in their silence. I wanted to come from outside, from my farm or from 35,000 feet—directly, without a shade of arrogance, on a par, as happy as they to be singing—with the good earth for my roots and a whole sky for my branches and winds from elsewhere and silence and the freedom of solitude.

I can be alone in a crowd—flanked by it, but with my head and my lair to myself. But now, I no longer have a lair or a sky for spreading my branches. Now I'm all hunched together with no confidence in myself. Too close at hand they stifle me.

Nevertheless I liked the others, I still like them, without reservation. But what I really no doubt need to do is describe them. I can make them out better than they can themselves— as well as their solid roots and good substance. But their mere words cannot interest me unless it be by the meaning they convey despite themselves.

Thus in my book: "She wept, naïvely, over a lost piece of jewelry. . . . She already wept—without knowing it—over the death which separates one from every jewel. . . ."*

And here it's the same. All their actions go straight to my heart and I'm nearer to them than they are themselves. But now I lack space.

And therefore they bore me with their stories about jewelry. It's no longer a question of jewelry.

I only understand when I myself build up my branches. I can no longer express them if they stifle me. And what they express about themselves doesn't interest me.

I'll go to Vitrolles. I so much prefer the risk of death to the desiccation that I risk here. I find myself again as in Toulouse, but less solitary. I'm dying of the thirst for solitude. I'm a rotten

---

* Quotation from the first version of Saint-Exupéry's *Citadelle* (The Wisdom of the Sands).

machine, I need unknown foods. I'm crying out for help. I need so much to be enlightened. Enlighten me. What should one do in order not to die and in order to bear fruit. Where am I?

I'm drunk with goodwill—and like an orange tree I reach down into the soil. But an orange tree isn't very mobile. It's hard to change soils. I only have my dowser's instinct. I only know when I'm on the spot, but I never know where to go. I'm a very clumsy tree.

Letter to X[6]

Laon [late January 1940]

I came back from Paris demoralized; they need no one. One feels like the fifth person in a game of bridge. I felt much more useful on night guard duty at the airstrip. There was only me to deal with the telephone, the coded messages, standing watch; something depended on me and prevented me from going to sleep. And I could feel my heart beating. . . .

Letter to Léon Werth[7]

Laon [February 1940]

Dear Léon Werth,*

. . . It's freezing cold and I don't understand life very well, I don't know what to do with myself in order to be at peace. For at present we're no longer dealing with war. We were sent here in the expectation of events that didn't take place and so we are more or less resting. The others have earned it after losing their seventeen flight crews, but I've done nothing as yet, and if you find my war unreasonable, you'll find my rest—

* A good friend of Saint-Exupéry's to whom the *Letter to a Hostage* is addressed and to whom he was to dedicate *The Little Prince*.

which leaves me cold and comfortless—even more so. We live in a real "house" with a real dining room and a real central heating system; the songs ring false there and I no longer have to make up my wood fire at night. I liked that, I was cold but I felt myself the grand architect of the fire; I also loved my icy room at dawn. An icy bed is a wonderful thing, because if one doesn't move one lies in a warm river, but if one moves a limb one falls into an arctic current and the bed is full of mysteries with its Gulf Stream and its icebergs. In fact I dislike comfort that wipes out everything. I'm bored in "temperate climates." My nights here, between the radiator and the mirrored wardrobe, no longer convey that atmosphere of the bear hunt, and on waking I no longer have to cross that expanse of red tiles toward the fireplace, which I hesitated to cross because it made my teeth chatter with cold. And then there are the immediate missions that are nevertheless denied me, and you know that it wasn't the war that tempted me to undertake them. But among the comings and goings, the great sparseness and these bucolic attitudes, I need that which forces me to come out of my shell. And here I feel that I am inside an incubator. I understand nothing of this semi-luxury and I'm trying to leave Group 2/33 in order to join Group 1/52, which still carries on with its trade. In any case we're falling apart completely. Captain Guillaume has been transferred elsewhere and the group captain has been changed. Neither the songs nor the games have any point any longer. Léon Werth, you would be sad to see us again like this. . . .

I'd like you to know what in fact you know already; I very much need you, because first of all I think you're the one I love best of all my friends, and also because you're my conscience. I think I apprehend things as you do and you teach me well. I often have long discussions with you and—I'm not being partial—I nearly always agree that you're right. But also, Léon Werth, I like drinking a Pernod with you on the banks of the

Saône while munching a sausage with country bread.* I cannot say why that moment leaves me with a feeling of such perfect fulfillment, but I needn't say this since you know it better than I. I was so content that I'd like to repeat it. Peace is not something abstract—it is not the end of danger and cold, and I'm proud of myself at Orconte when on waking I heroically reach my fireplace. Peace means that biting into a sausage with country bread on the banks of the Saône with Léon Werth isn't meaningless. It depresses me that the sausage no longer has any flavor.

Come to see me, but we won't join the flying group, which is not exactly sad but depressing too. We'll go and spend the day in Rheims and try to find a good bistro. We'll call Delange† and tell him to bring Cam and Suzanne.‡ I invite you all to a big feast—come quickly to cheer me up. You have to hurry up, because if I join Group 1/52 I'll be very far from Paris.

Good-bye Werth, a warm embrace.

Tonio

I'll meet you at the Hotel d'Angleterre at Laon, near the station. The train journey takes two hours and twenty minutes—it's quite near. And there's a train arriving at 9:06 P.M. You can stay with me. I'll take the next day off to visit Rheims with you (I don't know the cathedral). Delange could join us for lunch or dinner and could drive you back to Paris. Would you like that?

Having invented an altimeter device which he patented in February 1940,[8] Saint-Exupéry was ordered to Paris to work at the

---

* Allusion to a lunch the two friends shared at Fleurville sometime around Easter 1939. This memorable moment is recalled in Part III of *Letter to a Hostage* (see below, February 1943). Léon Werth was to write later on: "*Letter to a Hostage* was written during the German occupation. A letter Saint-Exupéry wrote to me during the war is like a premonition of it."

† René Delange, whom Saint-Exupéry got to know as editor in chief of *L'Intransigeant* in the thirties.

‡ Wife of Léon Werth.

National Center for Scientific Research (CNRS). In a letter of January 22, 1940,[9] *the director of the CNRS had considered that it would be useful "for someone with a certain practical knowledge of flying and the necessities of aviation to be seconded to the Center's Directorate. Captain de Saint-Exupéry might be this person."*

In this connection Henri Alias* explains: "When the order for transfer to the National Center for Scientific Research reached the unit, Saint-Exupéry told me of the requests he had received from his friend Giraudoux, who wanted him to take on a propaganda mission to America, and of his doubts about accepting such an undertaking as he had not carried out any wartime flying missions. This led to his refusal."[10]

In the Squadron's Golden Book[11]

I was profoundly moved to find again, in the third squadron of Group 2/33, the youthful enthusiasm, mutual trust, and team spirit that some of us valued so deeply on the old South America line.

Everything is the same here, and what I value deeply in this squadron are the leaders who have remained young, the old professionals who have retained their simplicity, those fellow flyers who remain faithful, and that feeling of friendship that allows one to gather happily around an old, rather melancholy phonograph in an old shack, despite the danger, mud, and discomfort.

I am happy to be in Squadron 3.

Antoine de Saint-Exupéry

Feburary 11, 1940

---

* Commanding officer of Reconnaissance Group 2/33 from February 6, 1940.

Letter to his Mother[12]

[Orconte, April 1940]

My dearest Mama,

I did write to you and I'm sad my letters got lost. I've been rather ill (a very high fever with no apparent reason), but now it's over and I've rejoined my unit.

You mustn't hold my seeming silence against me, as I was in fact writing to you and rather miserable at being ill. If you could only know how much I love you, think of you, and worry about you. Above all I want my family to be at peace.

The longer the war and its dangers and threats for the future go on, the more I'm weighed down by worries for those who depend on me. I feel so sorry for poor little Consuelo,* who is left completely alone. If she takes refuge in the South of France, please receive her as a daughter for my sake.

Your letter made me very unhappy because it contained reproaches and I only want the tenderest messages from you.

Do any of you need anything? I want to do anything I can for you.

With fondest kisses,
Antoine

Flying Group 2/33
Postal Sector 897

Letter to his Mother[13]

[Orconte, 1940]

Dearest Mama,

I'm writing to you on one knee, waiting for a bombardment that has been announced but has not occurred. I'm thinking of you. . . . And it is for you that I fear.

* Saint-Exupéry's wife.

I receive no letters. Where on earth do they go? This hurts a little. This constant Italian menace hurts me because it places you in danger. I'm so miserable. I need your tenderness so much. Why must it be that all that I love is threatened? What frightens me more than the war is the world of tomorrow. All those destroyed villages and dispersed families. I don't mind death, but I do mind the spiritual community's being endangered. I want us all reunited around a white table.

I don't tell you much about my life; there's not much to tell: dangerous missions, meals, sleep. I'm terribly unsatisfied. The heart needs other employment. I'm very discontented with the preoccupations of the age in which I live. Accepted and experienced danger is not enough to calm one's conscience. The only refreshing spring I can find is in some childhood memories: the smell of burning candles on Christmas Eve. Nowadays, it's the soul that is a desert, dying of thirst.

I have time to write, but I'm not ready to, the book hasn't yet matured inside me—a book that should quench thirst.

Good-bye, Mama, a very loving hug.

Your own
Antoine

Saint-Exupéry, who had gone to Paris to consult a doctor, was told by René Delange on the phone during the night of May 10 of the German offensive.

On May 16, he was received by Prime Minister Paul Reynaud. Saint-Exupéry offered to cross the Atlantic immediately to try and persuade President Roosevelt to intervene. He argued that only a massive air-defense curtain could stop the German advance; and so planes had to be obtained where they were available (that is, in the United States). Reynaud refused Saint-Exupéry's offer, having already charged René de Chambrun with an official mission. Saint-Exupéry was deeply disappointed.

Group 2/33 withdrew to Nangis, then to Le Bourget and Fontainebleau, and finally to Orly.

In the following text,[14] Saint-Exupéry did in fact try to convince certain Americans that their country should enter the war. It dates from 1940 or 1941; the exact date is unknown.

To seek to grasp the world by means of an efficient conceptual system is part of the greatness of man's spirit. But one of his weaknesses is that he believes in it too much. When a scientist puts forward a theory, he does not immediately believe in its intrinsic value. He knows it is only a code to order the world and that order itself is valuable. The prime virtue of a theory is clarity, and a theory is cast aside if it results in more confusion than clarity, does more harm than good. And if we want to bring some order into human events on our planet, we must not let what is most precious to us be overshadowed or injured by our dispositions. The spirit must strive toward a synthesis that satisfies not just one of our needs—such as order or technical development—but all our needs.

. . .

How is it possible that at a time when the Germans were begging for bread, Holland, Sweden, and Belgium were leading autonomous lives? What is so different in the world now? Nothing—except the effects of surprise. The new concepts have so confused the world—as does any change of code—that we reacted too late and too slowly. It is obvious that if we had acted in unison when Germany entered the Rhineland,* we would have saved world peace, together with the balance of power and our honor. It is obvious that we could have saved it at the time

* In March 1936 the European powers did not react when Hitler decided to remilitarize the Rhineland.

of the *Anschluss* and perhaps even in Prague—although by that time it would probably have meant war.

It is obvious, striking, and irrefutable that we could still save it if a hundred million Germans found themselves faced with five hundred million Europeans, all alike, all united, all threatened with destruction in the name of the intolerable challenge their mere existence represents. It is not my intention to weigh here the grounds of this intolerable challenge, its sincerity or insincerity. I think Hitler is sincere. It is because he is sincere, like a latter-day Muhammad, that he must be destroyed. The existence of a free Holland is an intolerable challenge to a racist mind. And we are ready to die for a civilization in which happiness is not an intolerable challenge.

A hundred million Germans were ready to respect their neighbors only as long as the rest of the world guaranteed freedom. Every since the dawn of Christianity this solidarity has operated, more or less effectively, with intermittent injustices and eclipses. Liberty, inner peace, human respect, are a priceless treasure, but a treasure that can only be universal. If cowardice, fear, and avarice prevent the world from uniting to defend it, then this common treasure is lost.

We who know how to be rich in that which all others possess, we who glory in individual faces, we who do not need to stamp the same imprint on all the five hundred million female faces of this globe, we who are rich in the diversity of the world and the individual happiness of others, we who while defending our happiness are above all defending the happiness of others, because the happiness of others is our own—if the others do not unite, it is because they do not understand. It is so obvious that there is a Russian, a Dutch, a Scandinavian, a Norwegian soul. How could this ever cease to be so, since it has lasted for so long? . . . They once again make the common error of mistaking for an eternal and unchangeable part of humanity's essential biological makeup something that is in fact a conquest of the human spirit, an inner habit. They cannot imagine that the things they lived for could disappear. They cannot believe, with their little horizon of happy people, that something essential could disappear, that a whole spiritual realm is threatened. They do not believe in major historical upheavals that obliterate all trace of previous generations and entirely transform continents. They do not believe that what seems to them unjust is possible. They protest by being stunned, by worshipping in secret, by appealing to God's justice, as if such treasures could be preserved without loss, as if culture did not have to be freely transmitted from generation to generation.

We know that we can fight above all for France because we are Frenchmen, but beyond that for the French way of life, for the Swiss cantons, the Dutch tulips, and the Norwegian dream. We may fight for them without their knowing it, and though their fate is in our hands they do not even dare say it for fear of being the first to be devoured by the ogre. They cannot be protected by guarantees and do not wish to draw attention to themselves, but they, the Austrians, Czechs, and Poles incorporated into Nazi Germany, can only shout *Heil Hitler* and hide their real wishes. These are weak and can be excused for trying as long as they can to save their heritage, which would otherwise be crushed—perhaps unintentionally—by enemy squadrons. We know what it is to fight for the weak and do not expect them to step forward in order to become the first victims of the enemy. But you, who are the voice of an enormously powerful country protected by the oceans, powerful in its navy, army, and fighting men, you who have nothing to fear, should it really be your role to tell your countrymen to wash their hands of any involvement, like Pontius Pilate? There is much to be said about this. This war does not directly threaten your survival, but it concerns you nevertheless. Perhaps it concerns the Nazis even more, because it is a religion that we fight for: freedom, which is also your religion—because it is a spiritual attainment that we defend and that you also share. Even if you inhabit another continent, you nevertheless inhabit the same planet and are heirs to a civilization where men show solidarity, where if Messina, Tokyo, or San Francisco is destroyed by an earthquake, you do not differentiate: You suffer for Messina, Tokyo, and San Francisco. You would help the people of Messina to rebuild the city even though Messina is Italian, you would not punish it further, because Messina is not Nazi. You are like us and like those whose fragile existence lies in our hands and who cannot express their secret wishes except in prayer, who do not covet their neighbor's land or possessions, and who have long ago cast off and stowed away the trappings of the Roman emperors. England is much more powerful than Holland, yet it does not covet the Dutch colonies. France is much more powerful than Switzerland and yet does not covet its French speakers. You are incomparably more powerful than Mexico and yet you do not covet Mexico. You are among those who have gradually emerged, ever since war ceased to be a glorious outing, where the noble emotions aroused were perhaps worth the few lives it cost, and became a giant charnel house, where man is crushed under the weight of machinery— you have emerged to turn it into a new wonderfully hopeful concept, namely the stability of empires. Let there be an end to games that have become too dangerous to be played, that destroy more than they save! An end to territorial ambitions! If we do not all want to die in the mud, we must make peace someday.... There are so many conquests open to man!

It is ideas that divide, not explain, the world, and your way of thinking—if it proves unalterable—will damage the world we love. If your way of thinking spreads, then we are truly buried in the debris of our individual creeds. But a line of thought is judged by its success, and its success is not linked to something transcendental but to its rigorousness. One could contrast your slightly simplistic reasoning with another, more fertile sort that promises greater hope. Your arrangement can be contrasted with another, which, if it gathers together more shining faith and energy, will enable us to win out.

I went to Germany and questioned physicists. One can no longer consider physics today without taking into account Einstein's equations. Is one allowed to read Einstein? Certainly not. Those who need to know Einstein's equations in order to understand the world have to spit on Einstein if they do not want to ignore him.

Germany was a great nation of scientists but is now merely a nation of technicians. You know how human thought progresses: By means of free contradiction, there emerges a focal point at which a theory and its opposites intersect. When the discomfort becomes too acute the over-tight mold cracks. Then comes someone who sees beyond the contradictions and arrives at a synthesis. Freedom alone allows human thought to progress. And for two hundred years we have watched humanity's conquest of nature. But suddenly a man appears who petrifies thought, rigidly confining it in a straitjacket, and suddenly, under his iron fist, humanity is reduced to the status of an anthill. Thought can no longer progress because it cannot contradict itself. Suddenly it is overshadowed by the specter of Truth, an intangible yet granite-like monolith that built gigantic anthills in the past as well.

. . .

Perhaps Hitler has—more than others—known how to reap the benefit of our knowledge and the scientific expertise of his country. He has known how to produce the arms you admire and how to plant his talons in his people. But where can one see grandeur in this? I only see a marauder looting the fruits of human thought, of despised human thought. An "intellectual" in Germany today is synonymous with a foolish dreamer or dangerous theoretician. Ensconced in the temple of knowledge, they plagiarize any works offered and devour what they would have been incapable of creating. We who fight for ourselves first, but also for all those who think as we do—we who fight for you, too, since we fight for your heritage—we also fight for Germany, for the Germany that you admire and against the marauders who have turned her into a fortified camp. You well know that we seek nothing but the right to live in peace. We fight for a fundamental luxury, which, erroneously, we considered natural since it seemed so evident—for a luxury that we did not know needed defending. How could we have guessed that the fanatic next door would discover the monstrous fact that he who is alone has no right to his clothes since he is unable to defend them against others? We are fighting for humanity, so that the individual should not be crushed by the mass, so that a painter should be able to paint even if he is not understood, and a scientist experiment even if he seems unorthodox. We fight for all fathers and their sons—in order that tenderness may preside over the family table, in order that sons may not denounce their fathers to a party official—in order that friends should not betray, and in order that he who is weak, protected by law, protected by universal convention, may keep his clothes even though he is unable to defend them.

But for this a universal convention is necessary. All men must jointly defend this possession. Every man must be a part of his own nation, empire, spiritual heritage, but also a part of mankind and ready to defend each human being against the mass.

General Order "C" No. 44 of the Air Force[15]

June 2, 1940

Commanding General Vuillemin, Commander in Chief of the Air Force, cites: . . .

Captain Saint-Exupéry, Antoine Jean-Baptiste Marie Roger, pilot with R.G. 2/33. Grounds:

"Flying officer of the highest intellectual as well as moral qualities, always volunteers for the most dangerous missions. Has brilliantly carried out two photographic reconnaissance missions. On May 22, 1940, violently attacked by intense anti-aircraft fire, did not break off his mission until his plane was severely damaged. A model of devotion to duty and self-sacrifice for the other members of the unit."

Between June 4 and 8 the defensive line of the Somme and Aisne under General Weygand was penetrated.

On June 10 began the population's dismal exodus southward. Saint-Exupéry speaks of these hordes of civilians thrown onto the roads in Flight to Arras.

The Reynaud government established itself in Bordeaux on June 14. Paris was occupied the same day.

Saint-Exupéry was in Bordeaux on the 16th. For two days he talked to those who still maintained an appearance of steadfastness; but it was too late to halt the irresistible course of events.

On June 17, Marshal Pétain formed a new government. He requested an armistice and, on June 22, obtained it.

On June 3, the six remaining flight crews of Group 2/33 withdrew to Nangis. Then on the 10th, they received an order to make for Chapelle, Vendommoise, Châteauroux, then Jonsac and Bordeaux, and finally the airport of Maison-Blanche at Algiers.

Letter to his Mother[16]

[Bordeaux, June 1940]

My dearest Mama,

We're taking off for Algiers. I love you and embrace you.

Don't expect any letters, as that will be impossible, but remember that I love you dearly.

Antoine

In a letter written during the summer of 1943, Saint-Exupéry told the story as follows: "Personally I was against the armistice. I stole an airplane at Bordeaux. I squeezed forty young pilots—recruited by me in the streets—into it (it was a four-engine Farman) and took them off to continue the war in North Africa. I was then unemployed!"

Letter to X[17]

[Algiers, early July 1940]
I've just heard this moment that a plane is leaving for France—the first and only one. Nothing leaves for France from here—neither letters nor telegrams.

I'm sadder than you could possibly imagine.

Many things, too many things disgust me.

I feel like a malfunctioning part, and in this morass one can only bite one's nails in exasperation.

I did what I could as well as I could.

I'm in despair.

One day, no doubt, we'll return. . . .

Saint-Exupéry was demobilized at the beginning of August and returned to France on board the Lamoricière.

He settled at Agay near his family, and began work on what was to become The Wisdom of the Sands.

During the summer, somber threats accumulated. The new government together with the German authorities initiated measures against the Jews. In particular, the "Jewish Statute" came into force on October 3. It was during these sad days that Saint-Exupéry went to see his friend Léon Werth.

Firmly convinced that America would intervene in the war sooner or later, Saint-Exupéry wondered whether he would not be most usefully employed there because of his double role of writer and aviator.

Contemplating going to the United States via Lisbon, he wrote to Vichy in order to obtain the necessary visa.

The Vichy government, eager to enlist great names in sports and adventure in order to further its youth policies, was considering offering the famous flyer a post in the Ministry of Education.[18] These propaganda moves, totally foreign to Saint-Exupéry's ideas, later gave him a great deal of trouble.

At the beginning of November Saint-Exupéry arrived in Algiers. He went to visit his comrades of Group 2/33, based at the time at El Aouina, near Tunis.

At the end of November, after embarking in Tangier, Saint-Exupéry arrived in Lisbon: "A sort of bright yet sad paradise," he would call it in Letter to a Hostage. *He wanted to embark on one of those rare ships that still sailed for America.*

On November 27 he heard of the death of his friend Guillaumet, whose plane had been shot down over the Mediterranean.

Once again he felt distressed and hesitant.

Letter to X[19]

Le Palace, Estoril, Portugal
[December 1, 1940]

. . . Guillaumet is dead and tonight I feel I have no friends left.

I don't pity him. I've never been able to pity the dead, but it'll take me so long to come to terms and I'm already burdened by this heavy labor. It will take me months and months: I'll be needing him so often.

Age overtakes us so speedily! I'm the only member of the old Casablanca–Dakar team remaining alive. All those who knew the grand old days of the *Breguet XIV*: Collet, Reine, Lassalle, Beauregard, Mermoz, Etienne, Simon, Lécrivain, Wille, Verneilh, Riguelle, Pichodoux, and Guillaumet—all are dead, and I've no one left on earth with whom to exchange reminiscences. I've become a toothless old man who ruminates over these things by himself. And not one remains of all those on the South America route, not one. . . .

I have not a single comrade left to whom I can say: "Do you remember?" What a perfect desert. Of the eight most intense years of my life, there remain only Lucas, who was only an administrator and joined us late, and Dubourdieu, with whom I never shared quarters, since he never left Toulouse.

I believed this only happened to very old people, to find that they have lost every one of their friends along the way.

The whole of life has to be begun again. Try to help me see the landscape, I beg of you. I'm in despair at being on the downward slope.

Tell me what to do. If I should come back, I will do it. . . .

At the beginning of December 1940, Saint-Exupéry left Lisbon for America. He made the crossing on board the Siboney, *a little ship of the American Export Lines, together with the film director Jean Renoir.*

On December 31 he was welcomed in New York by his friend Pierre Lazareff.

1941

Recollections of Lewis Galantière*

What actually persuaded Saint-Exupéry to leave France and exile himself among us is a question I never put to him directly. He had friends and a great reputation in the United States, of course. His books were very popular and he was sure to have no material worries in this country. But we were a neutral power, the French were a defeated and humiliated nation; and with the best will in the world the American people could not be expected to share the ceaseless gnawing anxiety by which he, as a Frenchman, was then beset.

I have never known a man so little made for neutrality, for

* Lewis Galantière translated several of Saint-Exupéry's books into English, including *Wind, Sand and Stars* and *Flight to Arras*. He published his reminiscences of the author in "Antoine de Saint-Exupéry," *The Atlantic Monthly*, April 1947.

emigration, for exile. Saint-Exupéry was obsessed by the notion that France must stay in the war. He wanted passionately to serve his country, but as a soldier, by fighting for it. As early as September, 1939, he had refused to lend his pen to the French propaganda ministry and had insisted upon serving as a pilot though he was in his fortieth year.

In January Saint-Exupéry settled in New York at 240 Central Park South.

His political dilemma surfaced immediately. Jean Renoir, who saw a lot of Saint-Exupéry in New York at this time, testified to this:[1] "He did not seem in the least attracted to Gaullism, being much more worried about the situation in occupied France. . . . Saint-Exupéry and I were in agreement: It was easier to be a hero in New York, far from the fight, than in France under the German jackboot."

When he heard that he had been named (without having been consulted) a member of the National Council, an assembly of notables set up in Vichy, Saint-Exupéry had no way of refusing except by making a statement to the press on January 31, 1941.

The Gaullists later reproached him because of this appointment. He was deeply hurt.

Hesitant on his arrival in New York, Saint-Exupéry did not remain there out of conviction. He was forced to stay, on the one hand by his literary commitments, and on the other because of his health problems, which were to necessitate an operation.

At the end of spring 1941, he went to Hollywood to stay with Jean Renoir. He underwent two operations.

During his convalescence he worked on Flight to Arras *and* The Wisdom of the Sands, *reread Andersen, and thought about* The Little Prince.

During June in Los Angeles, Saint-Exupéry met Professor Theodore von Karman, a theoretician of aerodynamics, who the following year was to write to a colleague: "I have just seen Antoine de Saint-

Exupéry, who explained his ideas on aerodynamics. These ideas are very novel and capable of revolutionizing our science."[2]
On June 22, Germany attacked Russia.

At a dinner in New York during the spring of 1941, Lewis Galantière grievously misinterpreted a sentence of Saint-Exupéry's concerning Aéropostale.
Saint-Exupéry loathed misunderstandings. That evening, on returning home, he immediately wrote a letter to his American friend in order to clarify his meaning.

Letter to Lewis Galantière[3]

[Spring 1941]

Dear Lewis,

Forgive this letter, but any confusion always makes me feel desperate. I'd like to correct a conversation that went off on a tangent halfway through.

I said to you that blowing over the admirable Aéropostale there had been a breeze of democracy that had spoiled everything. Obviously if I'd been writing, I would have avoided that dangerous word. For me the term contained in short form a number of facts that I thought were clear. I used it in its negative sense, not being concerned with its noble meaning in this connection. I wasn't speaking of democracies; I didn't say, "As Daurat is against democracy, democracy is to be discarded." I said, "The reproaches that are usually—justly or unjustly—leveled at democracies are those that I mean and which in my opinion led to the degeneration of Aéropostale." If in horror at the Saint-Sulpice style of religious art, I say: "This kind of religiosity disgusts me," if in a given society I criticize the despotic nature of the clergy, if I attack a scholar for sectarian dogmatism, I denounce something so obvious that even the most fervent believer would not dream of being offended. It's obvious that I'm speaking neither for nor against the existence of God.

In this way I could be the most ardent of democrats and still declare unequivocally that democratic tendencies destroyed Aéropostale.

When you gave the word I used an importance that quite naturally opened a new chapter in the discussion, I was doubly distressed—first of all because afterward I was unable to lead the discussion back to what I basically wanted to tell: the history of the destruction of Daurat's work.* I'm unhappy when I go off on a tangent; still, it was my fault this story was lost. I allowed these destructive undercurrents to be identified with something that sincere men die for, and I could no longer express myself without cutting that arbitrary and incidental link. Thus, if I criticize Fabre's religious dogmatism and am then accused of denying the existence of God, I shall have to abandon the problem of instinct in order to discuss that of knowledge, which is quite another matter. Conversations that veer off at a tangent always disconcert me.

Moreover, this new turn in the discussion led me on to sad perspectives—polemics. And polemics upset me much more even than conversations that go off on a tangent. And you, who are so openminded in discussing anything—there is one subject and one subject only into which you introduce polemics. But I'll first define the word "polemics."

You always have the right in any discussion to insist that I clarify my views, to point out my contradictions, and to demand that I resolve them. In the same way I have the right to demand that you define democracy. Strict as these demands are and serious as their possible rejection may be, there is no question of polemics here. Polemics begin when you no longer demand clarity on my part but instead use my lack of it to triumph over me; where you no longer wish me to specify, being only too

* Daurat was Saint-Exupéry's superior at Aéropostale.

happy to exploit my erroneous choice of words in order to show me up as being in the wrong; where you no longer wish to know what I wanted to express but only use what I said. If I despair every time that I see polemics ahead, it is because I know only too well that words in conversation, when not carefully weighed and qualified, only achieve their object if they meet with a receptive understanding. One can always get the better of all verbal statements. . . .

But these tripping-up tactics have nothing to do with the search for truth.

You rarely refuse me the receptive understanding that chooses for itself, among many possible meanings, the one that was intended. *I can only make my meaning clear in a conversation on condition that you wish me to be clear.* But there is one subject which—as soon as it is broached—turns you into a polemicist, and that is democracy. Every time that word has been mentioned in meetings between us, you have tried not to listen to me, but to put me down. You have always preferred me to be unclear.

I know what I mean when I speak to you of democracy. But your reaction, which has always stymied me from the start, making me stumble over my words, always prevented me from finishing what I had begun to say to you.

You have always opposed me, not by expressing yourself in a clear statement—which you never did—but by a kind of intuitive indictment. I have never criticized the nature of that indictment, or more precisely, the nature of the universe that would emerge from it if it were openly expressed. An intuitive indictment can be neither right nor wrong, neither logical nor illogical. It is what the impulse is to the sculptor. It will be worth what the sculpture is worth—or the statement.

Such an impulse is integral and must be set forth in an integral language. But this is a creative process, for my impulse is not yet the sculpture of a sculptor nor yet the statement of a sociologist. There is no logical path from one to the other. There is no rule that allows someone swayed by a strong emotion that is obviously present to construct a poetical image that will enable you to experience it. The poetical image is compelling, but there is no clear link between the impulse and the creation of a compelling image.

I therefore deny nothing of the indictment that so obviously makes you [illegible] to me. I also know that my impulse is real and can therefore be stated, and that it could become a valid religion if I show myself capable of growing a tree out of the seed (that is, of transforming a shapeless impulse into a finished piece of sculpture). I know that once this has been accomplished, my impulse will communicate itself to others besides myself. It will convert, exactly as the poetical image converts the reader to the poet's emotion. But I also know that such a statement is not mere reading or translation, but a difficult undertaking. And I know that you are wrong when you think that you have made your indictment by using the word "democracy," or by referring to the currently accepted definitions of democracy. You are just as mistaken as a writer who, having put suspension points at the end of a sentence in order to signify his emotion, imagines he has communicated it and is indignant if I'm unwilling to confuse his dots with a mode of communication. I know an adorable woman named Hortense. "Hortense" means something to me; for me the word is filled with emotion. But I do not pretend to overwhelm you by saying "Hortense."

For all those who know Hortense, nevertheless, those two syllables will mean the same thing. For all those who feel the need to make an implicit indictment, the word "democracy" will carry the same weight. However unsatisfactory the description of Hortense is, they will be moved by it. However broad your statement on democracy, it will allow you to express yourself to others like you, since you were all alike to begin with. The word is merely a rallying sign and the statements are of no importance. When in 1917 some right-wing French officers, prisoners of war in Pomerania, sang the words of the *Marseillaise*, they felt a link beyond the words, for the words could scarcely have suited them.

But if you imagine you can move a single foreigner by pronouncing the word "Hortense," you will fail. If you imagine you will convert a single unbeliever by your statements on democracy, you will again fail. You will only convert the converted. You will not even strengthen their faith, and the only thing they'll be able to do to preserve it is to probe as little as possible into the meaning of your words and to ask no more of your statements than the right-wing officers asked of the *Marseillaise*.

You'll have the illusion of expressing yourself because you'll have a preexisting audience. You will be speaking of Hortense to her suitors. But don't project your inner self onto others. The others don't care a damn. An idea that doesn't present an image men are ready or even eager to die for is worth nothing. Don't confuse "passion for democracy" with the instinct to identify, which is common to all humanity: "Let us be allowed to remain as we are. . . ." Nobody wants to be nazified, or exiled, or mutilated, or moved out, or woken up at night, or sent to prison, or forced to cut their hair differently, or deprived of Coca-Cola. For you, "democracy" stands for (though it fails to capture) a strong and vital inner impulse. Your passion beautifies words that may be transitory or outdated. You cannot doubt your own inner truth. You feel—quite rightly—that you could "explain" what is meant. You also know that there are followers who feel like you. But it is wrong of you to add to those adherents all those who are merely reluctant to change their habits. That is a swindle, because those masses of people are ready to take up any religion on condition that they are offered words they find compelling. And here "compelling" means either resolving contradictions or awakening and satisfying aspirations. Your language lacks this power. It is a rallying cry, not a vehicle.

As a true language of commitment, yours is dead. Not that

the thing you're talking about is dead; it isn't dead, indeed, it may be only just emerging. It is neither precisely Christianity nor an encyclopedic conception. What is dead is the old language, the moldering synthesis that this old language pretends to bring about.

It is difficult to analyze this without long reflection. I can only sketch a superficial and debatable critique. I accept in advance all the reproaches you may voice against this statement. I only want to say that the words that you invest with an emotional value, as I do in the case of the name "Hortense," are not as simple or as clear as they seem to you. Let us take, for example, the French concept of "Liberty–Equality–Fraternity." I choose this concept because it was used by you in a lightning attack against my timid reservations.

I've no idea how you define liberty. There are innumerable possible definitions. There are some in the light of which the present age appears as one of the most "limiting" in history. My present liberty rests only on mass production, which stultifies all dissident desires; it is the liberty of the horse whose harness shows only one path. The liberty to do what, good Lord, in my bureaucrat's rut? It isn't very original to follow a present-day Babbitt's footsteps, to watch him buy his morning newspaper, digest the ready-made thoughts in it (the fisherman and the mountaineer evolve their own), choosing one of three opinions proposed to him, then make a 50-degree turn of the screw shunted along to him on the conveyer belt, lunch at a drugstore where no allowance is made for any individual wish, then follow him to the movies, where Mr. Zanuck crushes him under his dictatorial stupidity, and finally see him go to bed with his wife or off to watch the baseball game on his day off. But no one is horrified by this ghastly liberty, which is only the liberty not to be. True freedom lies only in the creative process. The fisherman is free when he fishes according to his instinct. The sculptor is free when carving a face. It is a travesty of freedom to be free to choose between four models produced by General Motors, or between three films by Zanuck, or between the twelve items offered at a drugstore. Liberty then becomes nothing more than the choice of an article among a number of standard articles, all alike. I give the condemned a choice between being impaled or hanged and I admire him for being free! Give me the rules of chess quickly so that I can improvise, a road map so that I can go anywhere, a rooted man so that I can free him!

In fact, if I look for an example of true freedom, I'll only find it in a monastery, where men have a choice between different impulses chosen from the richness of their inner life.

Equality? I only see it clearly in the Catalan anarchists' doctrine. In fact, it can only be and is only the crushing of man by the mass: Einstein will be waiting at the post office at the end of a line of laborers. I'm ready to acknowledge that ideal, but you yourself aren't ready to acknowledge it. In the end, if you think about these words, you'll discover that your egalitarianism is in direct opposition to your freedom. Either my freedom is the freedom to resemble everyone else and is based on the amputation of all that differs: I cut off a man's legs and then allow him to go wherever he wants; or else my freedom is the freedom to differ, and in that case I no longer know how to define it. I know what the equality of two triangles means, but I don't know what the equality between a triangle and an apple means. Equality only means something when it applies to comparable objects. Equality and liberty really agree together only in an anthill. Once the stardard robot has been established, it is equal and free. You may free a white ant, but it won't make a fuss about it. It will rush back into slavery.

But it is fraternity that makes for the most inextricable problems. What you call fraternity is a well-wishing indifference that takes no real interest in anyone. I have known true fraternity only in the family hierarchy. There I heard the tenderly uttered "my younger brother" or "my elder brother." Have you ever heard anyone say "my brother" in the United States? Those feelings are seldom to be met with. You have lived too long in European families to dispute this. In America the degree of closeness between brothers is more or less the same as that between second cousins twice removed in Europe.

As far as brotherhood among men goes, I've only met it under Daurat and in war, where men were subordinated to something beyond themselves, ultimately dependent on each other, and hierarchically placed like the cells of a tree. Men can be brothers only within a greater framework: the family, religion, the defensive line, their country. But if something is transcendent, it organizes and thus destroys equality. Equality is found and is no doubt definable only within mutual transcendence. Captain and soldier are equal in the eyes of their country. One could say that that inequality is the necessary precondition for fraternity. Neither Daurat nor the war are examples of freedom. (Or rather they are the only examples of true freedom that I have been privileged to experience, for freedom needs to be defined.)

Your fraternity is therefore in opposition to your liberty and your equality. Your liberty itself is in opposition to your equality. These words had a meaning when they were used to oppose something else, or to bring about a change. They meant something at a certain living moment, something that could never be expressed in purely political terms. They are now empty shells, sonorous concepts of no meaning. They now equate with something like "It is desirable that everyone should be content." Having said that, one has not got very far.

Once again, no part of your inner indictment is questionable, but nothing is contained in those words. One can always—if one tries—concoct some meaning for them from among the thousand possible meanings, the thousand possible interactions, and you would certainly furnish me with an acceptable one. But this selecting and discarding is the sculptor's work and requires your presence. I can always pretend to convert you to my views on Hortense by numerous descriptions, but it will need my intervention to portray what it all signifies, to help you imagine one face out of 100,000 possible faces. These words do not make up a poem that conveys, converts, and rules. That poem remains to be written.

Once upon a time those words were a fertile seed. The tree has grown, but it is dead. That is the fate of any synthesis. Another seed is needed.

Then your definition of democracy must no longer cover the merry-go-round of French governments, the restrictions on all creativity, the standardization of man, the refusal of any transcendental restraint upon people, instead lumping them together in the same mold to establish their fraternity (because your democracy implies that work is merely an object for barter, which is absurd). Nor does it cover the lack of meaning in our daily behavior, which reduces our inner life to sordid poverty. If, someday, American youth, tired of baseball, discovers primogeniture, which makes for brothers, the inflexible orthodoxies that impart the rapture of apostleship; if they demand the constraint of rules in order to enjoy the pleasures of a game, what will you have offered them in exchange?

Perhaps, according to you, they lack nothing. But I refuse to consider the fact that people are satisfied with what they have as a proof that they lack nothing. There is no absolute instinct that makes one demand something as yet unconceived. But if one makes people aware of an inner impluse that exalts them, then they will demand to know what the conditions for it are. You can't try to love your brother more than you already do. There's no point to such a wish. Such a way of thinking is impossible. But once one has tasted the intensity of an inner life that contains brotherly love, one desperately demands the conditions that create it. The crowd does not know—cannot know—that it is bored. Boredom is merely a form of regret. The cavemen, who were already biologically like ourselves, did not regret Bach or miss baseball. But beware of seeing that boredom taught to the crowd. Nazism would spread among American youth like wildfire. The young are at loose ends. You may then try to combat this, but you will have at your disposal mere empty words and an inner conviction more attractive and more exalting than degraded Nazism, but because of a lack of preparation and creativity you will be unable to convince others. Your youth will espouse what it is offered. They will take up as their bible the first poem that stirs them.

I'm aware that you'll criticize my remarks about your youth; nevertheless, I'm right. They have no chance to be sons, brothers, or lovers, or to lead a mystical life, or to know love of a mother-country (America is a continent rather than a mother-country). All that remains to them is the chance to be democrats, that is, according to you, to love what they are. That is all that democracy means to them. And the problem remains unsolved.

Antoine de Saint-Exupéry

Letter to X[4]

Los Angeles [September 8, 1941]

I've changed since the war. I've acquired a complete contempt for everything that interests *me*. . . . I'm curiously sick, almost all the time, sick with a total indifference. I want to finish my book—that's all. I exchange myself for that. It is fixed to me like an anchor. I shall be asked in the next life, "What did you do with your gifts and how did you influence your fellow men?" Since I did not die in the war, I exchanged myself against something other than the war. He who helps me toward this is my friend, and the only possible help is freedom from strife. I need nothing, neither money, nor pleasures, nor company. I have a vital need for peace. I seek no personal end, no approval from public opinion. Everything now is a struggle with myself. It will be published only after my death, for I shall never finish it. I've already amassed seven hundred pages. If I worked at these seven hundred pages as I would on an article, it would take me ten years just to prepare a final draft. I will just work at them while I can, to the exclusion of all else. As for myself, I'm meaningless and can't understand why I'm an object of controversy. I feel threatened, vulnerable, limited by time—I want to complete my tree. Guillaumet is dead and I want to finish my tree quickly. I want to become something other than myself, and quickly. I'm no longer interested in myself. My teeth, my liver, and the rest are moldering away and my body is of no intrinsic interest. I want to be something different when it is time to die.

Perhaps all this is trivial. I don't care if it is thought trivial. Perhaps I'm wrong about my book, perhaps it'll be a long mediocre book—I don't care. It is the best I can become. I must become better—better than if I were killed in the war.

For the first time I wasn't much upset by the rubbish in the newspapers.* Before, I would have been unable to work for a month. But at present I don't care what judgments are made about me. I'm in a great hurry, a very great hurry, and I no longer have any time to listen to all that. If it's better now for me to die, I would be quite ready to die somewhere; only I've found a vocation I consider more worthwhile. So it's over. I now think that my vocation lies in what I do, whether one is for or against me. I have learned through the war and Guillaumet's death that one day I shall die. It was no longer the poet's abstract idea of death, which is a sentimental event and wished for in distress, but something quite different. Nor was it the wish for death of a teenager "disillusioned by life." No, it was the idea of a man's death—irrevocable death—life at an end. . . .

* The affair of Saint-Exupéry's nomination to the National Council set up by the Vichy regime.

Letter to Lewis Galantière[5]

[November 1941]

Dear Lewis,

Here is a short note, the first I have written. I am sending it to you so that you may be a link with our friends Reynal and Hitchcock. I hope you will be able to read it—I have lost the habit of holding a pen and am too nervous to form regular letters.

First of all, here are some details about this complicated business and about an operation that may have been as unnecessary as treating the foot in order to cure the head.

I must tell you that for some time now, I have been more and more frequently ill with an inexplicable illness. I felt no pain anywhere, and then, suddenly, I would wake up at night shivering as if I were having an attack of malaria, with a temperature between 104 and 105. It was absolutely exhausting. It was also incomprehensible, as I didn't have malaria and there was nothing wrong with any of my organs.

When I said in New York, "I have been ill, I have had a temperature of 41 degrees," nobody felt sorry for me, because nobody understood that 41 meant a temperature of 105. . . .

The only indication they had concerned the gallbladder, which they wanted several times to remove. As I felt little pain there, this theory did not strike me favorably and I steadfastly refused to undergo the operation.

But I have found an intelligent fellow here who furnished me with a tempting explanation of my symptoms. And I succumbed to it. I must tell you that I had three bouts of fever with a temperature of 105 within a week at Jean Renoir's. It became unbearable.

Here is the tentative diagnosis. (Alas, it is still only tentative.) In 1923 I was involved in a severe plane crash (spinning into the ground) in a wooden plane. After half an hour's effort I was dragged out of the wreck with a fractured skull, a fractured sternum, a fractured wrist, and a certain number of holes. The holes were caused by splinters of wood, especially splinters from the seats.

The fellow's theory was as follows: These violent bouts of infectious fever, which cannot be due to a diseased organ since I have none, could very well be accounted for if one were to discover a pocket of scar tissue going back to my old accident, which periodically becomes infected.

After various examinations and X rays, it seemed that such a mass of scar tissue existed. It impeded no function, but seemed destined to be a more or less permanent cause of infection. It was therefore decided to remove this tissue.

I agreed to the operation, because there was no question (as in the case of the gallbladder) of removing a useful organ for a hypothetical advantage. I would lose nothing by the experience and I might gain by it.

But it is no fun. The operation provoked a series of unbearable spasms during my convalescence, as well as minor bleeding and one or two bouts of fever. Moreover, I have an eye that has had the bad habit of becoming inflamed—from any infectious cause whatever—ever since I fractured the bone near the optical nerve. An infectious embolism deriving from a foot injury in Saigon, an inflammation of my arm, injured in Guatemala—everything has caused a recurrent internal hemorrhage in this stupid eye. Nor has this time been any exception. So on top of everything else I had an infected eye. It was treated with the help of violent artificial bouts of fever of up to 105.6. And now things are better.

But all this has worn me out. I still suffer a lot from the spasms (which are, however, diminishing) and I'm just beginning to get up. All in all, I feel very low. I also wonder whether I was right to allow myself to be cut up in a part of my body that caused me neither trouble nor pain, and I fear that I gave in to an ingenious but far-fetched idea.

I am no doubt wrong to feel doubtful, as the doctor who treated me seemed very competent. And in any case something had to be tried.

This kind of operation, which takes so long to cure, due to bleeding and recurring infections, sets one's nerves on edge. My Guatemalan injury was less painful. I think that at last things are improving.

Please forgive me for being late with my book. I am more desperate than you. Since I hope to have begun my real convalescence at last, I hope to regain that inner peace of mind and nerves, which alone enables one to work. How lucky are those hewers of wood and drawers of water who are not dependent on their inner climate where their work is concerned.

This is not a proper letter. I am too much under the weather still. I am incapable of telling what I want to tell you. These lines are just intended to inform you about my state of health, which I was unable to do earlier and am still only able to do badly.

You will have a tough time cheering me up.

Yours affectionately,
Saint-Ex

Letter to Lewis Galantière[6]

[November 1941]

Dear Lewis,

I leave on Sunday. I'm better and I'm even hopeful of being rid of the bouts of sickness which have been poisoning my life for the last three years—and with increasing frequency—and which, alas, were not in the least of nervous origin! No nervous breakdown wakes you up at three in the morning shivering, with chattering teeth and a temperature of 104 to 105! No nervous breakdown is stopped dead by sulfonamide, which is specifically applied in cases of septicemia and made me able to function in the afternoon with a just tolerable nausea and temperature.

But this medicine, which helped me out each time, is a dangerous one. On the other hand, if I had been without it, what would I have done? During the whole war, I carried some in my pocket in case I was captured.

The fact that my attacks were of infectious origin was proved by all the tests; white blood corpuscles, etc . . . (and also by the characteristic shivering). That is why, in the absence of any indicative pain, all the doctors wanted to remove my gallbladder, since it was the only organ that caused me any pain. But I considered the pain too slight when compared with my violent bouts of fever and always refused to have the operation performed. I wanted more conclusive proof.

As time passes, I believe more and more in the explanation given me here. On my arrival in California I had three bouts of fever within a week; since then, however, although I'm feeling low after this painful operation, overwrought and racked by innumerable worries—among them my unfinished book—I haven't had another attack of fever since the operation, despite a few passing complications.

Of course there were months without bouts of fever and the final proof will depend on the long-term results. But during the last few months, these attacks were very frequent, and their nonrecurrence for a month now seems a good sign to me.

I tell you all this because you seem to think that I've been treating the vague ills of a neurotic little girl, whereas it was a question of specific, violent, and repeated attacks of fever, which— had sulfonamide not existed—would have kept me in bed for two weeks and perhaps finished me off. And what a life! If my flying group had known of these bouts of fever, they would have sent me back to my studies instead of putting me in charge of a plane and flying crew. Unable to complain of these attacks without being forcibly relieved, I carried out high-altitude missions with a high fever. I even had to invent a fictitious story about malaria when I was caught unprepared during a bout of fever at a medical checkup, although, despite my years in the colonies, I managed to escape that plague.

If you had no idea I was ill, it was because the sulfonamide kept me going, more or less. But if you had seen me a few hours before, shivering, with chattering teeth, you yourself would have forced me to let a surgeon try something. And I might then have lost an almost healthy gallbladder that fascinated the medical profession in the absence of any other indication.

By the way, they didn't remove one scar just to replace it with another; they removed an abscess. (In fact they exchanged a vertical scar for a horizontal one.)

I think all doctors would agree that the existence of such an abscess . . . constitutes a permanent cause of serious infection that can spread . . . to the kidneys. Anyone discovering this abscess, and unable to drain it, would have decided to operate.

Please forgive me for carrying on about my illness. I don't usually do so and I don't think I've spoken much of my ills when measured against all the trouble I've had. But I've spent three years keeping back all those insoluble worries, years so unbearable that you must forgive me if I break my long silence! (Do you remember that dinner at the 21 Club with your niece? I left in order to get back to work. It was a lie. I left because I felt a bout of fever coming on and could hardly stand up!)

Dear Lewis, I'm fond of you. I promise never again to hold forth in this senile way. I feel bad, but all this has worried me so much that I must get it off my chest. I'll now get back to my book, the title, the war, Europe—and friendship, dear Lewis.

Saint-Ex

On December 8, 1941, one day after the Japanese attack on Pearl Harbor, America entered the war. On December 11, Germany and Italy declared war on the United States.

At the request of the journalist Dorothy Thompson, Saint-Exupéry gave a speech before a group of student volunteers from the Progressive Education Association.[7]

A Message to Young Americans

Dorothy Thompson has asked me to say a few words to you, and I am happy to do so. Here I do not feel like an author addressing an abstract public. I feel that I am sitting among you, young people of goodwill, as one of you, in order to ponder problems which mean a great deal to us all. But above all I speak to you as I should like to speak to my own people, who are far away. Be my friends.

You are at war. You are young. You are prepared to work and fight for your country. But there is more at stake than your country; it is the world's fate that is at stake. And you are ready to work and fight for freedom the world over.

If you were just soldiers, I would speak to you as soldiers. I would say: "Put aside all other problems, there is only one that counts: fighting." But you are young and your responsibility is greater even than that of soldiers. Yours is a dual responsibility: You are ready to fight for liberty, but you must also explain it and build it.

Words too much used lose their meaning. Social formulas wear thin. That is the price of humanity's advance. If you do not want to live by dead ideas, you have to rejuvenate them constantly. But liberty is not a problem you can separate from others. In order for human beings to be free, they must first be human. Therefore you will find that the basis of all problems is the problem of man.

Freedom, liberty, can mean many different things. It may be the freedom to cut yourself off from your customs, to give up your traditions, to lose interest in your community, as long as you do not injure anyone. You might say that "individual liberty ends where it wrongs another." And you do not injure your neighbor if your social life consists of exchanging work for bread. You have only received your due. Your absence would change nothing. But your absence, even if it does not injure your neighbor, injures the community, for it is poorer without you. It is necessary to enrich the community, since it alone enriches man. One is a member of a country, a profession, a civilization, a religion. One is not just a man. A cathedral is built with stones; it is made up of stones; but the cathedral ennobles each stone, which becomes a cathedral stone. In the same way, you will only find brotherhood in something larger than yourselves, because one is a brother "in" something, not merely a brother. People need to find a bond between them. This bond may be specific. Hunchbacks may establish the sect of hunchbacks. He who is not a hunchback is excluded. But the pride of Christian civilization—from which we originate and which is ours, whether we believe or not—is to seek this bond in the universal, not the particular.

Nazism tried to define the German or, more laboriously, the Aryan, in order to make him into the object of an exclusive religion. We try to define man in order to build ours. Our whole civilization has sought, first and foremost, to define man. When you demand of the most famous and most valuable of doctors that, despite his importance, he should risk his life by attending to a contagious person, you do not subordinate the doctor to another individual but to humanity, which the contagious person represents, whatever his failings. If you want to free the word "democracy" from all the misunderstandings that sully its visage, then remember that liberty here means respect for mankind, and that if you want to introduce brotherhood into democracy, the community of man must be built not on the exaltation of the individual but on the submission of individuals to the cult of humanity.[8]

And so, there is only one way to construct a being far larger than yourselves, which in its turn will enrich you by its existence. The oldest religions discovered this long ago. It is the basis of all religious and social thought. It is the supreme "trick," which has been somewhat forgotten since the advent of material progress. That "trick" is sacrifice. And by sacrifice I mean neither renunciation of all the good things of life nor despair in re pentance. By sacrifice I mean a free gift, a gift that demands nothing in return. It is not what you receive that magnifies you, but what you give. That which you give to the community builds the community, and the existence of the community enriches your own substance.

Man's urgent need to free himself from slavery by securing for himself the fruits of his work has centered attention on labor as an exchange value, on labor as a commodity. But we must not forget that one of the essential aspects of work is not the salary that it brings in but the spiritual enrichment that it procures. A surgeon, a physicist, a gardener is more human than a bridge player. One part of work feeds you, the other builds you; it is the dedication to work that builds you.

This is the way in which Dorothy Thompson invites you to give of yourselves. She invites you to build your community. When you take in the harvest without pay for the good of the United States at war, then you are helping to build the community of the United States. And the same applies to your brotherhood.

I would like to cite my own experience:

For eight years I lived the life of an airline pilot. I had a salary. Every month I could buy some goods I wanted with the money I had earned. But if my life as an airline pilot had brought me no other advantage besides these material ones, why should I have loved it so much? It gave me much more. But I must admit that it only truly enriched me when I gave more than I received. The nights that enriched me were not those in which I spent my earned salary, but those in Buenos Aires, at the time when the postal air routes were first started, when I had fallen asleep exhausted after flying for thirty hours without sleep and a sudden phone call, due to a far-off accident, would get me out of bed: "You must go to the airfield. . . . You must fly to the Straits of Magellan. . . ." And I got out of bed grumbling.[9] I filled up on coffee to keep from falling asleep while flying. Then, after an hour's drive along rough, bumpy dirt roads, I would reach the airfield and meet up with the other fellows. I shook hands without saying a word, still half asleep, crotchety, stiff from the rheumatic pains that winter weather brings on after two sleepless nights. . . . I got the engine started. I read the weather forecast as a set chore: storms, frost, sleet . . . and I flew off into the night toward a doubtful dawn.

But when I weigh the feelings left in my heart by the events of my life, I find that only the memory of these tasks counts. Their shining path surprises me and I remember that feeling of being comrades-in-arms in the hours of the night. I discover with surprise that the hands I shook while grumbling have left me with a memory of deep affection. The search for lost comrades, the forced landings for repairs in rebel territory, the utter exhaustion, that aspect of action that cannot be reckoned in terms of payment—now I discover that this was what stirred me, though at the time I was unaware of its power. But the memory of the nights spent squandering my salary is nothing but ashes.

I never got anything that mattered out of my work when it was only something to be exchanged against a pay scale measured in kilometers of a pilot's flight. My work meant nothing if, while feeding me, it did not also make me part of something: pilot of a specific airline, gardener of a specific garden, architect of a specific cathedral, soldier of a specific country. If creating new airlines enriched us, it was because of the sacrifices that it demanded of us. The airlines were built with the free gift of ourselves. Once born, the airline gave us birth. If today I meet a comrade, I can say, "Do you remember . . .?" It was a wonderful time when, bound by the same free gift of ourselves, we loved one another.

Antoine de Saint-Exupéry

"My first offense," Saint-Exupéry *wrote to his friend Sylvia Hamilton, "is to be living in New York while my people are at war and dying. . . . Why won't they let me climb back into a warplane again? . . ."*[1]

In January 1942 Saint-Exupéry was putting the finishing touches on Flight to Arras. *His correspondence with his translator reflects the author's irritation at the demands of his publisher, especially the deadlines for delivery of his manuscript.*

Letter to Lewis Galantière[2]

[January 1942]

Dear Lewis,

Please forgive the ill humor my letter will seem to express. It's not directed against you. I feel deep affection for you. But I'm in a towering rage, which must come out.

What is this nonsense about a deadline? Why must I constantly come up against a date that is anything but absolute, since if I had begun writing six and a half weeks later the date would have been fixed for six and a half weeks later, with the same logical arguments?

Why should I sell myself short and slight my work—which comes down to the same thing? I believe the carpenter should plane his board as if it were essential to the earth's rotation. This applies even more to writing. Why should I sell myself short because of a stupid question of dates, telling myself: "If I were Pascal, my text would deserve to be worked on and I would have the right to express myself. But as I am only myself, no one cares if I express myself, and the hack from the *New York Times* takes precedence over me. As for my book, it is nothing and I am very vain to be so concerned about it!"

If I write, I must ask myself, What will they think of my book? What will be its fate in ten years' time—not what will one possibly cross-eyed and infantile individual think of it on February 22—an individual I don't give a damn about anyway. I don't care in the least whether a poem I write and like is read or heard forty years after my death. The image of the misunderstood poet, condemned to penury by man's injustice and not rehabilitated until a hundred years later, has always seemed to me the most foolish sentimentality. On the contrary, the poet is very lucky. I won't weep over the eels that spawn in the Sargasso Sea and will never know their offspring.

Either my book is good and will be read one day—I don't care when—or else it is worthless and will have only a moment of topical interest, and then I don't care a jot whether it is read or not.

There is the question of money. I need money, etc. I need it badly and I'm delighted when I get any, but I cannot mix up these two considerations. I merely have two forms of egotism, one of which greatly exceeds the other. I couldn't buy anything with money that meant more to me than the pleasure of saying what I mean. If I express myself badly for the purpose of getting money I do myself a disservice.

I prefer the sale of a hundred copies of a book I don't have to blush for to the sale of six million copies of a bad book. This is justified egotism, because the hundred copies will carry much greater weight than the six million ever could. The belief in numbers is one of the fallacies of the age. It is the most select journals that are the most illuminating; the *Discourse on Method*, even if it had had no more than twenty-five readers in the seventeenth century, would nevertheless have changed the world. *Paris-Soir* with its yearly tons of paper and its two million readers has never changed anything.

It will perhaps seem foolish to you that I say all this about a largely anecdotal tale (I've no illusions about its interest for the world at large)—but the objection means nothing to me, as I should feel the same way if I had been writing on horticulture. One is present in a book and should present oneself honestly.

Don't tell me I'm wrong because my manuscript is "ready to go" and I won't be making any major changes. I won't make any great changes in the essential message—that's true—but I'll greatly change its impact. This is not a question of the material or the surface narrative. It's something that only begins to exist when one no longer sees why. And I know exactly what changes to make. They involve something that I can't define, which concerns the lasting quality of what I say. If *Wind, Sand and Stars* still sells, it is because I cut it drastically when I came to the United States. I know that. I've written too many articles to be unaware of this. It is never the immediately apparent that counts. Whenever I hear an echo, years later, from an article of mine in that ephemeral commodity, a newspaper, it is always, always, always an article that I rewrote thirty times. When I read a quotation of my own somewhere, it is always, always, always a phrase I rewrote twenty-five times. One sees no very noticeable difference between the first and last versions. It may even be that the final version seems less picturesque, but it is bound by an inner logic. It is a seed; the other was a plaything for a day. I have never, never, never been wrong about that.

I agree with you that just because I may think more clearly in ten years' time is no reason to wait ten years. Agreed. One must express oneself in the present, but it is precisely in the present that I haven't expressed myself. Today I'm worth more than my book. Therefore it is unforgivably cowardly not to be part of my book. On what grounds should I skimp my work? I freely admit that there are limits set to the writing of a slim volume, but in what way—may I ask—have I overstepped decent limits? I have not even spent eight months on this text— which was (for me) a record.

If your reading of the manuscript was more favorable today than the other day, it will be more favorable still tomorrow. The book has a limit. That limit is what I am today in 1942. You would have the right to think this limit reached only if two successive versions more or less tallied with each other. This was not the case today. By what means can you tell that this version represents me fully? If anyone can detect the discrepancy, it can only be me.

There remains the problem of France. If it's a matter of the number of readers, that's not important, and I don't care. An opinion is not the opinion of the "greater number." An opinion passes by osmosis from one person to another. One reader can be fully sufficient.

If pressing topical interest is the issue, then I understand even less. That's a complete illusion, because the topical interest of the day after tomorrow will be very urgent too. And what about the topical interest of the end of March 1957! It will be very pressing for the people of 1957. For the people of 1957 it will—wrongly perhaps, but mercilessly—take precedence over the topical interest of 1942. Why should I prefer one to the other? On the day I die, when I lucidly look at the balance sheet and objectively weigh matters up, I won't give preference to either. Besides, I have irrefutable proof: I have no regret—nor any reason to regret—that my book was not published a week, a month, six months, or a year ago. What matters is today. What will be important in a week's time will be an entirely new today.

Oh, Lewis, you do cause me a lot of anguish.

Saint-Ex

Letter to Lewis Galantière[3]

[January 1942]

Dear Lewis,

... The end makes me despair. They are forcing me—God only knows why—to substitute a foolish journalist's write-up for a statement of where I stand. I know what I have to say, and it's vital to me. I know I could convey it by setting out simple arguments that would convince naturally without seeming to. Why—for the sake of an absurd deadline—must I provide a banal statement instead of my real object, or attempt to convey that by means of arguments that are still contradictory and ineffectual? The way—the only way—is to arrive at a point of view that puts things in their rightful place and from which the author disappears. A point of view is not seen—one has arrived at it. A truth that is not "a point of view" is valueless or paradoxical and convinces no one. And what's more, it's deadly, and for good reason. That serves no purpose.

Do you think I like having to substitute a piece of nonsense for what I wanted to say about responsibility, just because of lack of time? If I had found the right words, nothing would have shocked you. You would have found yourself faced with such simple facts that it would have seemed to you that you had discovered them yourself; you would have been my prisoner for the rest of your life without knowing it—yes, I really believe for the rest of your life.

Instead of that, you are justifiably shocked by an utterance so incoherent and contradictory that it is indecent of me to present it. It is like exhibiting a dead fetus; while I—full of remorse and failing to understand the importance of April or May '42—scrap what I had to say in order to present a valid statement that I might have put forward at the age of five. What is the use of overcoming illnesses, accidents, exams, female entanglements, tax problems, and worries of all sorts, if it all leads to my repeating—without progressing one jot—what my nanny already taught me? I see no urgent need to propagate in 1942 what she knew perfectly well in 1900. That could wait until the year 2000. It might then be thought original because almost forgotten.

I'm dog tired. I've written 200 pages in six days and it gets me no further. Nothing can replace time. Time is needed to grow pears, to raise children, to elaborate points of view. The next time I write for Reyhitch,* I'll write a short story, the love story of a blonde and a hussar. If Lamotte† lends a hand, it'll be marvelous.

I'm really down in the dumps. It is 7 A.M.

> Your friend,
> Saint-Ex

Recollections of Lewis Galantière

The book [*Flight to Arras*] was published, in English translation, in February, 1942. A man who publishes in New York, two months after Pearl Harbor, a book in which he declares that the important question is not "What ought we to do?" but "What ought we to be?" is bound to seem to Americans a mystic or a madman. It did not occur to us that Saint-Exupéry was writing for the French, and that their Pearl Harbor had taken place twenty-one months earlier, in May, 1940. On the other

---

* Reynal and Hitchcock, his American publishers.
† The illustrator Bernard Lamotte.

hand, Saint-Exupéry was at fault in forgetting that he had started to write a book for Americans, and that his American readers were faced with a situation which was not to be resolved by essays on the moral nature of man. He ended by writing for the French, a people whose morale needed support after a humiliating defeat. He published among the Americans, a people whose only thought was how to organize and employ the resources they must bring to bear if they were not to suffer a defeat no less humiliating.

Two months after Pearl Harbor, at a time when Laval was about to return to power at Vichy, American readers wanted Saint-Exupéry to write about Democracy with a capital D: he wrote about Man. They wanted him to celebrate the Bill of Rights: he sang the beauty of Charity. They asked him to announce to them—like Heine in "The Two Grenadiers"—that the French Army was about to rise up out of its grave, sword in hand: he brought them tidings of the immortality of the substance, the "seed" as he put it, of France. Only the French, in 1942, were in a mood to appreciate *Flight to Arras*.

First published in three installments in the Atlantic Monthly, Flight to Arras, *the English version of* Pilote de guerre, *translated by Galantière and illustrated by Lamotte, came out in the United States on February 20, 1942. It stayed on the best-seller list for six months.*

Letter to X[4]

[February 1942]

My dear,

I need very much to see you again. I'm tired. I've taken a heavy load upon myself and there can be no question of living in peace by ridding myself of it, nor of being able to breathe while bearing it. What a curious thing conscience is! . . .

And now my little volume will come out. And, as usual, all the slanders and jealousies are being prepared. You can imagine the mafia of pseudo-French in New York who are already coming forward. I sense the mud stirring. . . . Oh, how sad, discouraged, and tired I am!

Here is my book. Believe me, I don't think well of it. I wrote it in an inner turmoil. I didn't succeed in saying what I wanted to. I beg you to send me a cable when you have received and read it. I'll phone you immediately. But let me know a word by cable. If you think it terrible, do say so—I have no vanity.

I embrace you, my dear.

Antoine

At the end of November, Saint-Exupéry made a radio appeal that began with the words "Above all, France!" The text appeared in French in the Montreal newspaper Le Canada *on November 30, 1942,[5] an English translation having appeared in the previous day's* New York Times Magazine *under the title "An Open Letter to Frenchmen Everywhere." The appeal went out on the air from all American radio stations broadcasting in French and was reprinted in the North African newspapers.*

An Open Letter to Frenchmen Everywhere

Above all, France! The German night has swallowed up the country. For a time we were still able to know a little about those we love; we could still send them words of affection, even if we could not share the wretched bread on their tables. From afar we could catch their breathing.

All that is over now. France is nothing but a silence; she is lost somewhere in the night with all lights out, like a ship. Her mind and spirit have been absorbed into her physical being. We shall not know even the names of the hostages who tomorrow will die before the German rifles.

It is always in the cellars under a tyranny that new truths are born. Let us not play the part of braggarts. There are forty million people over there in France who must endure their slavery. We shall not be carrying any fire of the spirit to those who are already nourishing the flame with their life's blood— like the wax of a candle. They will deal with French problems better than we can; they have all the right to deal with them. Our talk about sociology, politics, and art will carry no weight with them. They will not read our books, they will not listen to our speeches. Perhaps our ideas may make them sick.

Let us be infinitely modest. Our political discussions are the discussions of ghosts; ambitions among us are comic. We do not represent France; all we can do is to serve her. And whatever we do, we shall have no just claim for recognition. For there is no common measure between being free to fight and bearing the crushing weight of the darkness. There is no common measure between the métier of the soldier and the métier of the hostage. The people over there in France are the only true saints. Even if we have the honor of taking part in the battle, we shall still be in their debt. There, in the first place, is the fundamental truth.

Men of France, let us be reconciled in order to serve!

I shall say a few words about the quarrels which have divided Frenchmen in the hope of doing something to remove them. For there has been a grave spiritual disorder among French people. The souls of many among us have been torn; these have need of peace of mind, and they should find it. By the miracle of American action in North Africa, all our different roads have led us to the same meeting place. Why now should we get bogged down in the old quarrels? It is time to unite, not to divide, for opening wide the arms, not for exclusions.

Were our quarrels worth the hate we wasted on them? Who can ever maintain that he alone is absolutely right? Man's field of vision is minute; language is an imperfect instrument; the problems of life burst all the formulas.

We were all in agreement as to our faith. We all wanted to save France. France had to be saved both in the flesh and in the spirit. Of what use is the spiritual heritage if there is no heir? What good is the heir if the spirit be dead?

All of us hate the idea of collaboration. Some of us accused France of real collaboration while others saw only a ruse. Let us think of Vichy as a trustee in bankruptcy, negotiating with a greedy conqueror for delivery to France of a little grease for railroad cars. (France can no longer get gasoline, or even horses, to bring food to her towns.) The officers of the Armistice Commission will one day tell us about this persistent and atrocious German blackmail. A quarter-turn of the key—delivery of any less grease than required—and a hundred thousand more French children would die in the next six months.

When a single hostage is shot, his sacrifice shines forth. His death is the cement that binds French unity. But when the Germans, by merely holding up an agreement on grease for cars, kill a hundred thousand hostages of five years, where is the compensation for this slow, silent hemorrhage? What is the acceptable fixed price for dead children? What would have been the tolerable limit of Vichy's concession in its attempt to save them? Who can say?

You are aware that French denunciation of the armistice terms would have been equivalent to a return to a state of war. It would have justified the conqueror's seizure of all adult males as military prisoners. This blackmail lay heavily over France. The threat was plainly set forth. German blackmail is no jest. The rot of German prison camps yields only corpses. My country was thus threatened, purely and simply, with utter extermination, under legal and administrative presence, of six million men. France was armed only with sticks to resist this slave hunt. Who is in a position to say for certain what should have been her resistance?

Here at last is the seizure of North Africa by the Allies within sixty-six hours to prove, perhaps, that in spite of blackmail and in spite of two years of pressure, Germany has failed seriously to encroach upon this North African territory. Somewhere, then, there must have been attempts at resistance. Perhaps the victory in North Africa has been won, at least in part, by our 500,000 children who have died. Who would dare say that the number is insufficient?

Frenchmen, if we could reduce our differences of opinion to their true proportions, that would be enough to make peace among us. We have never been divided except on the question as to the weight to be attributed to the Nazi blackmail. On the one hand, some said, "If the Germans are determined to wipe out the people of France, they will wipe them out, whatever the French do. This blackmail ought to be despised. Nothing should make Vichy take such and such a decision or give this or that promise."

On the other hand, other people thought: "It is not merely a case of blackmail but of blackmail unique for cruelty in the history of the world. Let France, refusing all capital concessions, employ every sort of ruse to delay the menace from day to day. The tone of the official utterances shows that when a Ulysses or Talleyrand is disarmed, there remain to him only words with which to deceive the enemy."

Do you believe, Frenchmen, that these diverse opinions as to the rigors of the Nazi blackmail or as to the real intentions of this circumscribed government really ought to make us hate one another still? (When the English and the Russians fight side by side they leave to the future disputes which are grave enough.) Our divergences of opinion do not touch our hatred of the invader, while at the same time we are all indignant, as are all the people of France, at the surrender of the foreign refugees, a violation of the right of asylum.

Well, these quarrels of the past no longer have any point. Vichy is dead. Vichy has carried with it to the grave all its inextricable problems, its contradictory personnel, its sincerity, its ruses, its cowardice, and its courage. Let us for the time being leave the role of judge to the historians and the courts-martial after the war. It is more important to serve France in the present than to argue about her history.

The German occupation of all France has settled all our quarrels and brought appeasement to the drama of our consciences. Men of France, are you willing to become reconciled? There is no longer even a shadow of a reason for argument among us. Let us abandon all party spirit. Why should we hate one another? Why should we be jealous of one another? There is no question of positions to be won. There is no question of any race for offices. The only places open are soldiers' places—perhaps some quiet beds in some little cemetery in North Africa.

The military law of France binds all men up to age 48. From 18 to 48 we ought all of us to be mobilized. There is no question whether we wish to enlist or not. It is demanded of us, in order to turn the balance of war, that we take our places in the scale—all together and quite simply.

Although our old quarrels are now merely quarrels for the historians, there is another danger of disunion among us. Let us have the courage, men of France, to surmount this danger.

Some among us trouble themselves about the name of one leader as against another, of one form of government as against another. They see the phantom of injustice rising on the horizon.

Why do they thus complicate matters? There is no injustice to fear. None of our personal interests is going to suffer in the future. When a mason devotes himself to the building of a cathedral, the cathedral cannot injure the mason. The only role expected of us is a war role. I myself feel wonderfully safe against any form of injustice. Who could do me an injustice since I have only one idea—namely, to rejoin in Tunis my comrades of Group 2/33 with whom I lived through nine months of the campaign and then the brutal German offensive, which took two thirds of our number, and finally the escape to North Africa on the eve of the armistice? Let us not dispute now about precedence, about honors, about justice, or about priorities. There is nothing of all that offered to us. They are only offering us rifles—and there will be plenty of those for everybody.

If I feel so much at peace now it is because again I find in myself no leanings toward the position of a judge. The group of which I become a part is neither a party nor a sect, it is my country. I am not interested in who will command us. The provisional organization of France is an affair of state. Let us leave it to Britain and the United States to do the best they can. If our ambition is to press the trigger of a machine-gun we shall not be worried about decisions that will seem to us secondary. Our real chief is France, now condemned to silence. Let us hate parties, clans, divisions of any kind.

If the only desire we formulate (and we have the right to formulate it, since it unites all of us) is to obey the military leaders rather than the political leaders, it is like the military salute which honors not the soldier who is saluted but the nation he represents. We know what General de Gaulle and General Giraud think about authority; they serve; they are the first servants. That should be enough for us, since all the quarrels which weakened us yesterday are now resolved or absorbed in the present.

Here, it seems to me, we stand. Our friends in the United States should not get a false picture of France. Some regard

Frenchmen as a little like a basket of crabs. This is unjust. Only the controversialists talk. One does not hear those who keep still.

I suggest to all those Frenchmen who have up to this time been silent that they emerge from their silence just once to reassure Cordell Hull as to the true state of our spirit. I suggest that each of these send to him some such telegram as the following:

> We ask the privilege of serving in any way whatever. We desire the mobilization of all Frenchmen in the United States. We accept in advance any organization that may be deemed the most desirable. But hating any spirit of division among Frenchmen, we ask simply that the organization be outside politics.

The State Department will be astonished at the number of Frenchmen who will take their stand for unity. For, despite our reputation, most of us at heart know only love of our civilization and our country.

Frenchmen, let us become reconciled! When we find ourselves together one day in a bomber fighting five or six Messerschmitts, the thought of our old fights will make us smile.

During the war, in 1940, when I came back from a mission with my plane shot full of holes, I used to drink an excellent Pernod at the squadron bar. I often won my Pernod throwing dice, sometimes from a Royalist comrade, perhaps from one who was a Socialist, or perhaps from Lieutenant Israël, the bravest of our crew, who was a Jew. And we all clinked glasses in the greatest friendliness.

In December the Saint-Exupérys moved to 35 Beekman Place in New York.

Letter to an Unidentified Correspondent[6]

[New York, December 8, 1942]

I know why I hate Nazism—it is above all because it destroys the quality of human relationships. . . . I lived for years in the barrenness of the desert and I was happy there: I had faithful comrades. . . .

Oddly, the world these days is giving up what once constituted its greatness. . . . The Nazis, having turned the Jews into a symbol of baseness, extortion, treason, exploitation, and egotism, were honestly indignant at anyone's wanting to defend the Jews. They then accused their adversaries of seeking to preserve the spirit of extortion, treason, and exploitation in the world. Which takes us back to the age of African totems.

I reject those herdlike states of mind, those koranic simplifications; I refuse to invent scapegoats. I reject the Inquisition's good intentions. I reject the empty verbal expressions that uselessly cause torrents of blood to flow. . . .

I don't think highly of physical courage. Life has taught me that there is only one true kind of courage: resisting the condemnation of a mode of thought. I know that it took me much more courage not to budge from the line of conduct my conscience dictated to me despite two years of slander and insults than to photograph Mainz or Essen. . . .

1943

Jean Israël: My Book[1]

In a corner of my library a dirty, black, sad book lies hidden. Under its rough binding the dark gray pages are a witness to the vast number of dirty fingers that have turned over its pages.

The hands were those of a fraction of the eight thousand French officers herded together in a prisoner of war camp in 1943. This copy was the only one in the camp of a publication forbidden by the censorship.

Stamped with a magnificent seal *Geprüft* ("Examined"), it survived all searches and checks by the authorities. Its dilapidated state after a few months of circulation made me hand it over to the bookbinders. It was returned to me in serviceable order, bound in the material used for covering mattresses, and strong enough to withstand the next horde of readers.

This book was *Flight to Arras*, the first French edition, published on November 27, 1942 in Montrouge. Though it was at first allowed (censorship visa no. 14 327), permission was withdrawn a few weeks later. A copy bought in time by my mother and sent in a regulation food parcel was saved by a judicious theft in the barracks where the incoming mail was sorted.

Why this belated supression, when the book had received permission to be printed in France?

A review of the book by Pierre-André Cousteau, published in the weekly *Je suis partout*, got the ball rolling. In it Saint-Exupéry was referred to as a Jewish warmonger because he had praised "his friend Israël as a standard-bearer of French courage." This article was followed by a second even more violent one, resulting in the prohibition of publication and sale and the destruction of the stocks of the book.

Letter to a Hostage

While Flight to Arras*'s appearance in France was causing a tumult, Saint-Exupéry was composing* Letter to a Hostage. *The first part of this text was published in* L'Amérique Française *of Montreal in March. One hundred and twenty copies of the complete text were printed by Brentano's, Inc., in June.*

Jean Amrouche published Letter to a Hostage *in his journal* L'Arche *in Algiers in February 1944. Also in Algiers, the Information Service of the French Committee of National Liberation had it reproduced in quantity.*

In France the first edition was brought out by the publisher Gallimard on December 4, 1944.

Letter to a Hostage *was at first intended as a preface to a book by Léon Werth.*[2]

I

When in December 1940 I crossed Portugal on my way to the United States, Lisbon appeared to me like a bright, sad paradise. There was talk of an imminent invasion and Portugal was clinging to its illusion of happiness. Lisbon, which had put together the most exquisite exhibition in the world, smiled a slightly sad smile, like those mothers who haven't heard from a son at the front and seek to save him by their faith: "My son is alive because I'm smiling. . . ." "Look, how happy, peaceful, and beautifully illuminated I am," Lisbon said. The whole continent leaned over Portugal like a savage mountain weighed down by its predatory tribes. Lisbon—having a good time—defied Europe: "Can they choose me as a target when I so carefully refuse to hide? When I am so vulnerable!"

Our towns at home were dull as ash at night. I had got used to the absence of even a glimmer of light, and this brightly shining city made me feel vaguely uneasy. If the surrounding street is dark, the starkly lit-up diamonds in a shop window attract loiterers. One feels them moving along. I felt the European night inhabited by roving packs of bomber planes pressing down on Lisbon, as if they could have sniffed out this treasure from afar.

But Portugal ignored the monster's voracious appetite. It refused to believe in the threatening signs. Portugal spoke about art with despairing confidence. Would they dare to crush it and its cult of the arts? It had brought out all its treasures. Would they dare to crush it among its treasures? It displayed its great men. Lacking an army or cannon, Lisbon had set up all its sentinels of stone as a barrier against the invader: poets, explorers, conquistadors. For want of an army or cannon, Portugal's entire past blocked the way. Would they dare to destroy it in its heritage of a magnificent past?

Every evening, I wandered full of melancholy through the

triumphs of this exhibition in perfect taste, where everything was near perfect, including the discreet music, which wafted gently through the garden like the plashing of a fountain. Would that wonderful harmony of taste be destroyed?

I found Lisbon, under its smile, sadder than our own darkened towns.

I have known and perhaps you have known eccentric families who lay a dead man's place at their dining table. They reject the irreparable; but I did not consider this defiance a consolation. The dead must remain dead; then in death they acquire a new form of presence. But those families put off the return of their dead. They turned them into eternal absentees, guests forever late. They exchanged mourning for an empty expectation. Those houses seemed to me to be steeped in an uneasiness much more stifling and relentless than any grief. I agreed to mourn Guillaumet, the last friend I lost, who was brought down on a postal service mission. Guillaumet will never change. He will never be present again, but he will never be absent either. I sacrificed his place at my table—that useless snare—and made him into a true dead friend.

But Portugal was trying to believe in happiness, clinging to its place at the table, its lights, its music. They played at happiness in Lisbon, so that God should believe in it.

Lisbon also owed its atmosphere of sadness to the presence of certain refugees. I do not mean the outlaws in search of political asylum. I do not mean the immigrants in search of land to till. I mean those who left to get away from the misery of their fellow countrymen and to put their money in a safe place.

As I could not find a place to stay in town, I stayed in Estoril near the casino. I had survived intense fighting. My flying group, which for nine months had never ceased its raids over Germany, had lost three quarters of its men during the German offensive alone. On my return home I had known the deadly atmosphere of slavery and the threat of famine. I had known the blacked-out nights of our towns. And now just around the corner from me, the Estoril casino was thronged with ghosts every night. Silent Cadillacs pretending to be on their way to somewhere silently dropped them on the soft sand in front of the entrance. They were dressed for dinner as in bygone times. They showed off their stiff shirtfronts or their pearls. They had invited each other to a puppet meal where they would have nothing to say to each other.

They played at roulette or baccarat, according to their means. Sometimes I watched them. I felt neither indignation nor irony, but a kind of anguish—the same feeling that you experience at a zoo when looking at the survivors of an extinct species. They crowded around the tables, squeezed against an austere croupier, trying to feel hope, despair, fear, envy, excitement—just like living beings. They staked fortunes which were perhaps becoming worthless at that very moment. They used possibly obsolete coins. Their safes perhaps contained stock certificates backed by already confiscated factories or, threatened as they were by aerial attacks, already on the way to being destroyed. They drew bills of exchange on Sirius. They frantically tried to believe by linking up with the past—as if something had not begun to crack on earth a few months earlier—tried to believe in the legitimacy of their agitation, the honoring of their checks, the immutability of their conventions. It was unreal—it seemed like a puppet show. But it was sad.

No doubt they felt nothing. I left them to their own devices. I went for a stroll by the sea. And the sea at Estoril, this tame sea of a fashionable resort, seemed to me part of it all. A single soft wave rolled into the bay, shining in the moonlight like a ball dress out of season.

I met them again on board ship. The ship also exuded a feeling of anguish as it ferried these rootless plants from one continent to another. I said to myself: "I don't mind being a traveler, I don't want to be an emigrant. I've learned so many things at home that will be useless elsewhere." But now these emigrants were taking their address books out of their pockets, the remains of their identity. They still pretended to be someone. They clung obstinately to some semblance of meaning. They said, "That is who I am. . . . I come from such and such a town. . . . I am the friend of so and so. . . . Do you know him?"

They went on to tell you the story of a friend, or a mistake, or any other story that could link them to something. But nothing in their past could help them any longer, because they were emigrating. These memories were still warm, fresh, living, in the same way that recollections of past love affairs are fresh to start with. One gathers together a bunch of love letters. One adds a few recollections. One ties them together carefully. This relic at first has a certain melancholy charm. Then one meets a blue-eyed blonde, and the relic dies. Friendship, one's native town, recollections of home, also fade if they are not used.

They felt all this. Just as Lisbon played at being happy, so they played at believing they would return soon. The absence of the prodigal son is sweet. It is a fictitious absence, since the family home remains intact. There is no fundamental difference between being in the next room or on the other side of the planet. The presence of a friend who seems to have left can make itself more felt than an actual presence. That is the presence of prayer. I never loved my home as much as in the Sahara. No fiancés were as close to their sweethearts as the sixteenth-century Breton sailors rounding Cape Horn or growing old in the battle against contrary winds. As soon as they had set sail, they began their return. When hoisting the sails with their rough hands, they were preparing for their return. The quickest way to reach their sweetheart's house was via Cape Horn. But these emigrants seemed to me like Breton sailors who have been deprived of their fiancées. No humble Breton sweetheart any longer lighted a lantern in her window. They were not prodigal sons—they were prodigal sons without a home to come back to. There begins the real journey outside oneself.

How can one rebuild an inner hearth, how rewind the heavy spool of memories? This ghost ship carried creatures from limbo, souls not yet born. Only the crew and the personnel, at one with the ship and dignified by their specific tasks, carried trays, polished copper, cleaned shoes, and, with a certain contempt, waited on the dead. This contempt was not due to the emigrants' poverty. They lacked not money but weight. They were no longer people who had a certain house, a certain friend, or a certain responsibility. They only played that part, but it was no longer real. Nobody needed them, nobody would be appealing to them. What a blessing is the cable that gets you up in the middle of the night, sends you rushing off to the station: "Come quickly! I need you!" We quickly find friends to help us. We slowly become worthy of those who demand help. True, no one hated these ghosts, no one was jealous of them, no one bothered them. But nobody loved them with the only love that matters. I said to myself, "They will be invited to welcoming cocktail parties and consolation dinners as soon as they arrive. But who will knock on their door and shout, 'Let me in! It's me!' " One has to breast-feed a baby for a long time before it makes demands. One has to cultivate a friend for a long time before he takes it for granted. One must have been ruined keeping up a crumbling family mansion for generations in order to learn to love it.

II

And so I said to myself, "The essential thing is that something should remain of what one has lived for: customs, family celebrations, one's childhood home. The main thing is to live for one's return. . . ." And I myself felt threatened by the fragility of the distant poles on which I depended. I might well come to know a real desert, and so I began to understand a mystery that had long intrigued me.

I spent three years living in the Sahara. Like many others I mused over its magic. Anyone who has lived in the Sahara, where solitude and barrenness seem all-enveloping, thereafter cherishes these years as the most worthwhile he has known. The catchphrases about nostalgia for the desert or for solitude or for wide open spaces are nothing more than literary phrases and explain nothing. But here, on this ship, crammed with passengers one on top of the other, I seemed to understand the desert for the first time.

True, in the Sahara the sand or, more precisely, a stony expanse (dunes being rare) stretches away far as the eye can see. One is plunged permanently into conditions apparently conducive to boredom. And yet invisible gods endow the desert with any number of directions, slopes, signs, a secret and living relief, until there is no uniformity left. Everything finds its place. One silence even differs from another.

There is the tranquil silence when the tribes are at peace, when night brings coolness and one seems to be anchored with furled sails in a quiet harbor. There is the midday silence when the sun suspends all thought and movement. There is the deceptive silence when the north wind bears down, bringing insects borne like pollen from the oases of the interior and heralding the advent of a sandstorm from the east. There is the silence of conspiracy when it is known that a distant tribe is preparing to revolt. There is the silence of mystery when the Arabs are gathered together for one of their secret meetings. There is the pregnant silence when the messenger is late in returning, the shrill silence when in the night one holds one's breath in order to hear, the melancholy silence when one remembers one's beloved.

Everything is polarized. Each star shows a true direction. They are all stars of Bethlehem—each serves its own god. This one points to a far-off well that is difficult to reach, and the distance between you and the well is as heavy as a rampart. That one points to a dried-up well. The star itself seems dried-up. The distance between you and the dried-up well seems flat. Another star guides you to an unknown oasis that the nomads sing of, which a revolt prevents you from visiting. The sand that separates you from the oasis is a fairy-tale lawn. Yet another star points to one of the white cities of the south, as delicious, it seems, as a fruit you are about to eat.

Finally, almost unreal poles galvanize this desert from a great distance: a childhood home vividly remembered, a friend one knows nothing of, except that he exists.

In this way, you feel enlivened by magnetic forces that pull or push you, attract or repel you. Now you are rooted, set, established in the center of cardinal directions.

Since the desert has no tangible riches, nothing to see or hear, and since the inner life, far from diminishing, flourishes there, one is forced to conclude that man is motivated first and foremost by invisible attractions. Man is ruled by the spiritual. In the desert I am worth what my gods are worth.

If therefore I felt a sense of rich possibilities, if I inhabited a still living planet, it was because of a few friends left behind me somewhere in the French night who were about to become vital to me.

For me, France was neither an abstract goddess nor a historical concept, but something alive that I depended on, a network of bonds that ruled me, a set of axes that formed the structure of my heart. I needed to feel that those who were necessary to me in order to enable me to chart my course were stronger and more durable than I—so that I could know and return; so that I could exist.

My country was enfolded in them, and through them it lived on inside me. When you are at sea, a continent is reduced to a little illumination from a lighthouse. A lighthouse beam does not measure distance—its light is reflected in the eyes, that is all. All the continent's treasures are contained in that star.

Now that France, after the occupation of all its territory, has slipped into silence with all its cargo, like a ship without lights whose fate in the storm is unknown, the fate of those I love oppresses me more than any illness I have. I feel threatened at heart by their defenselessness.

The man who haunts my memory tonight is fifty years old. He is ill. He is a Jew. How will he survive the German terror? In order to imagine him still alive, I must believe the invader knows nothing of him, protected by the brave rampart of silence of the peasants of his village. Only then can I believe that he is still alive. Only then, as I wander at large within the empire of his friendship, can I feel like a traveler, not an emigrant. The desert is not where one believes it to be. The Sahara is more alive than any capital and the most teeming town is emptied if the vital poles of life are demagnetized.

III

How does life build the vital currents that we live from? Where does the magnetic force that pulls me toward this friend's house originate? What are the essential moments that made this presence into a vital pole for me? What are the secret events that mold particular affections and, through them, love of country?

How little stir the real miracles cause! How simple are the most vital events! There is so little to say about the instant that I want to recall that I have to relive it in a dream and speak to this friend.

It was on a day before the war, on the banks of the Saône, near Tournus. We had chosen to lunch at a restaurant whose wooden terrace overlooked the river.* Leaning on a plain table scarred by customers' knives, we had ordered two Pernods. Your doctor had forbidden you to drink any spirits, but you cheated on special occasions, and this was one of them. We did not know why, but this was one of them. It was something more impalpable than the quality of light that made us joyful. And so you decided on a Pernod for this grand occasion, and since two bargemen were unloading their barge nearby, we invited them over. We hailed them from the terrace and they came along. We had invited them quite naturally, as friends, perhaps because we felt an inner joy. It was obvious they would respond to our invitation, and we enjoyed a drink together.

The sun was warm. Its warm honey spread over the poplar tree on the opposite bank and over the plain to the horizon. We were more and more joyful, still without really knowing why. The sun shone reassuringly, the river flowed reassuringly, the meal tasted reassuring; the bargemen who responded to our invitation and the waitress who served us smilingly, as if presiding over an eternal feast, were equally reassuring. We were completely at peace, sheltered from disorder by a perennial civilization. We tasted a kind of bliss where, all wishes being fulfilled, we had nothing to confide to each other. We felt pure, righteous, luminous, and indulgent. We could not have expressed what profound truth was revealed to us, but we felt absolute certainty—an almost overweening certainty.

The universe was showing its goodwill through us. The condensation of nebulae, the hardening of the planets, the formation of the first amoeba, and the colossal task of nature from the emergence of the amoeba to man—all had converged happily to mature—through us—into this quality of pleasure. Not bad—in fact, rather an achievement!

* The Café de la Marine at Fleurville. See note to Saint-Exupéry's letter of February 1940 to Léon Werth.

We relished this wordless contentment, these almost religious rites. Lulled by the coming and going of the vestal waitress, we and the bargemen drank together like followers of the same religion, though we could not have named it. One of the bargemen was Dutch, the other German. The latter had long ago fled Nazism, having been persecuted as a Communist, Trotskyist, Catholic, or Jew. (I can't remember for which label he'd been outlawed.) But in that moment the bargeman stood for much more than a label. It was the contents that mattered— the human clay. He was simply a friend and we agreed among friends. All were agreed—but on what? Pernod, or the meaning of life, or the pleasantness of the day? We could not say which. But our agreement was so complete, so profound, and reflected such a solid though unformulated creed that we would gladly have agreed to defend this bastion, sustain a siege, and die behind machine guns in order to preserve the substance of that agreement.

What substance? That is very difficult to explain. I am in danger of capturing merely the reflections, not the essence. My feeble words will allow the truth to escape. I would seem obscure if I said that we were ready to fight for a certain quality in the bargemen's smiles, in your smile, and mine, and the waitress's, a certain miracle of the sun, which had taken such pains to shine for millions of years in order to arrive—through us—at this rarity, this rather well-executed smile.

Very often the essential is weightless. Here the essential seems to have been merely a smile. A smile is often the most essential thing. One is repaid by a smile. One is rewarded by a smile. One is animated by a smile. And the quality of a smile can make you die of it. However, since this quality has freed us from the anguish of the present time and granted us certainty, hope, and peace today, I need, in order to express myself better, to tell the story of another smile.

IV

It happened while I was writing a report on the Spanish Civil War. I had been imprudent enough to watch—clandestinely, at three in the morning—the loading of a secret cargo at a freight depot. The bustle of the people loading, together with the darkness, seemed to favor my indiscretion. But I became an object of suspicion to a group of anarchist militia.

It all happened very simply. I did not become aware of their stealthy approach until they had closed in on me softly, like the fingers of a hand. A rifle butt touched my stomach. The silence was ominous. Finally I lifted my arms.

I noticed they were looking not at my face but at my tie (such a curiosity being out of place in an anarchist neighborhood). My body tensed. I waited for the shot—it was a time of summary judgments. But none was fired. After a few seconds, during which the team of workmen seemed to be dancing a sort of dreamlike ballet in another world, the anarchists nodded to me to go ahead of them and we walked off slowly across the railway lines. The capture had been made in complete silence and with a minimum of movement—like the stirring of underwater plants.

Soon we came to a basement converted into a guardhouse. There was a little light from an oil lamp and the militiamen were dozing with their rifles between their legs. They exchanged a few words with the patrol that had brought me in. One of them searched me.

I speak Spanish but no Catalan. Nevertheless I understood that they wanted my papers. I had forgotten them at the hotel. I answered, "Hotel . . . Journalist," without knowing whether I was getting through to them. Each in turn looked at my camera. Some of those who were dozing roused themselves with a sort of boredom and leaned against the wall.

The overwhelming impression was of boredom. The powers of concentration of these men had been burned up. I would almost have preferred a sign of hostility as a means of human contact. But they showed neither anger nor disapproval. I tried several times to protest in Spanish, but my protests fell flat. They stared at me without reaction, as they would have at a Chinese fish in a fishbowl.

They were waiting. What were they waiting for? The return of one of their men? Dawn? I thought, "Perhaps they are waiting until they get hungry. . . ."

I said to myself, "They may do something stupid! It's ridiculous!" What I experienced was less a feeling of anguish than a disgust for the absurdity of it all. I said to myself, "If they react, if they want to act, they'll shoot!"

Was I really in danger? Were they still unaware that I was not a saboteur or a spy but a journalist? That my papers were at the hotel? Had they come to a decision? What decision?

I knew nothing about them, except that they shot people out of hand without any qualms. The revolutionary vanguard of any party hunt their quarry, but it is the symptoms, not individuals as such, that they pursue. Their opponent's truth seems to them a dangerously spreading disease. If they discover the smallest doubtful symptom, the patient is put in quarantine— the cemetery. That is why this vague monosyllabic interrogation that I could not understand seemed to me so sinister. A blind roulette wheel was deciding on my life. That is why I felt a strange need to call out something that would assert my existence—my age, for one thing. A man's age is something impressive, it sums up his life: maturity reached slowly and against many obstacles, illnesses cured, griefs and despairs overcome, and unconscious risks taken; maturity formed through so many desires, hopes, regrets, forgotten things, loves. A man's age represents a fine cargo of experiences and memories. Despite the pitfalls, the ups and downs, one has kept on advancing, lumbering like an oxcart. And now thanks to a lucky conjunction of circumstances, one was here—at thirty-seven. And the good oxcart—God willing—would continue further on its way with its load of memories. I said to myself, "This is where I've got to. I'm thirty-seven years old. . . ." I would have liked to weigh down my judges with this confession, but they were no longer questioning me.

Then the miracle occurred—a very discreet miracle. I had no cigarettes. Since one of my jailers was smoking, I asked him by gesture to give me one, and I smiled briefly. The man stretched himself, passed his hand across his forehead, lifted his eyes to my face instead of my tie, and to my utter surprise smiled back. It was like dawn breaking.

This miracle did not resolve the drama, it merely dissolved it as light dissolves shade. No drama had taken place—the miracle changed nothing visible. Everything remained the same: The old oil lamp, the scattered papers on the table, the men leaning against the wall, the colors and smells—all remained unchanged, but everything was transformed in its essence. That smile set me free. It was a sign as obvious and definitive in its consequences as the dawn is irreversible. It opened up a new era. Nothing had changed, but all had changed. The scattered papers on the table, the oil lamp, the walls were alive. The boredom exuded by the objects in the basement was lifted. It was as if an invisible bloodstream had begun to circulate again, binding the body together and giving it meaning.

The men had not moved, either, but whereas a moment earlier they had seemed as alien to me as an antediluvian species, they now seemed nearer to me. I felt an extraordinary sensation of "presence" and felt akin to them.

The young militiaman who had smiled at me and who a moment ago seemed a function, a mere tool, a sort of monstrous insect, now appeared a little clumsy and shy. It was not that he was less brutal than any other terrorist, but the manifestation of his human quality showed up his vulnerability. We men put on grand airs, but in our secret heart we feel hesitation, doubt, grief.

As yet nothing had been said, but everything was resolved. I put my hand on the militiaman's shoulder to thank him when he handed me the cigarette. And the ice once broken, all the militiamen became human and I entered into their smiles as into a new and free country. I entered into their smiles just as I had into those of the men who saved us in the Sahara. Our comrades, having found us after searching for days and having landed as near to us as possible, walked toward us with long strides, holding up their water bottles—which were clearly visible. The smile of the rescuers when I was stranded, or of the stranded when I was the rescuer, puts me in mind of a country where I was very happy. The real pleasures are the pleasures of companionship. Water has no power of enchantment unless it is a gift of human goodwill. The care of a patient, the welcome given to a fugitive, forgiveness itself, are only worthwhile because of the smile that goes with them. We meet in a smile above language, party politics, castes. We are followers of the same religion—the others with their customs and I with mine.

V

Isn't that joy the most precious fruit of this civilization we call our own? Even a totalitarian tyranny could satisfy our material needs, but we are not so many cattle to be force-fed. Prosperity and comfort cannot satisfy us. For those of us who were brought up in the creed of respect for humanity, the simple encounters that can sometimes change into almost miraculous experiences mean a great deal.

Respect for humanity . . . That is the touchstone! When the Nazi respects only what resembles him, he merely respects himself. He rejects the creative contradictions, ruins any hope of advance, and for the next thousand years replaces man with the robot in the anthill. Order for the sake of order emasculates man by removing his essential power to transform the world and himself. Life creates order, but order does not create life.

We, on the contrary, believe that our advance is incomplete, that tomorrow's truth derives from yesterday's error, and that the contradictions to be overcome are the very mainspring of our growth. We recognize that someone who differs from us is still one of us. But what a strange relationship—founded on the future, not the past, on the goal, not the starting point! We consider each other pilgrims who—along different paths—struggle toward the same goal.

But today, the very condition of our progress—respect for mankind—is in peril. The recent divisions in the world have led us into darkness. The problems are confused, the solutions contradictory. Yesterday's truth is dead and tomorrow's has yet to be created. No valid synthesis is in view and each one of us holds only one small part of the truth. Since they are not self-evident, political religions resort to violence. And now that we are divided as to the ways and means, we may forget that we are reaching out toward the same goal.

The traveler who crosses a mountain in the direction of a star runs the risk of forgetting which is his guiding star if he concentrates too exclusively on the climbing problems. If he only acts for action's sake, he will get nowhere. If I allow myself to be absorbed in party politics, I may forget that politics makes no sense unless it serves a spiritual certainty. In our privileged hours we have experienced a certain quality of human relations: There lies the truth for us.

However urgent the need to act, we must never forget the mission that must guide our actions, or they will all remain sterile. We want to establish respect for humanity. Why should we hate one another when we are all in the same camp? None of us has a monopoly on good intentions. I can disagree with someone else's course in the name of my own. I can question his reasoning. Reasons are never certain. But I must respect him on a spiritual level, if he is struggling toward the same star.

Respect for humanity! Respect for humanity! If such respect is rooted in the human heart, humanity will eventually establish a social, political, or economic system that reflects it. A civilization is before all else rooted in its substance. At first this was a blind urge for warmth. Then by trial and error man found the way to the fire.

VI

That is probably why, my friend, I have such need of your friendship. I need a companion who—beyond the struggles of reason—respects in me the pilgrim on his way to that fire. I sometimes need to feel the promised warmth ahead of time and to rest somewhere beyond myself in that meeting place that will be ours.

I am so tired of polemics, exclusivities, and fanaticisms! I can call on you without putting on any uniform, without having to recite any creed, without having to abdicate any part of my inner self. With you I do not have to exonerate myself, or plead a cause, or prove a point; I find peace as at Tournus. Beyond the clumsiness of my words, beyond my defective reasoning, you are ready to see me as a human being. You are ready to honor in me the representative of beliefs, customs, loves. If I differ from you, far from wronging you, I enrich you. You question me as you would a traveler.

I—who like all others want to be recognized—feel pure in you and am drawn toward you. I am drawn to where I feel pure. It was not my formulas nor my reasoning that taught you what I am. It was the acceptance of what I am that made you indulgent toward my formulas and my reasoning. I am grateful to you for accepting me at my face value. Of what use is a friend who sits in judgment on me? If I invite a friend to join me for a meal and he's limping, I do not ask him to dance but to sit down.

My friend, I need you as one needs the pure air of a mountain ridge! I need to join you again on the banks of the Saône at the table of a little dilapidated inn and to invite two bargemen to join us for a drink in peace and a mutual smile, as on that day.

If I continue to fight, it will be to some extent for you. I need you in order to be able to believe in the return of that smile. I need to help you to live. I see you—so weak, so threatened, dragging your fifty years behind you for hours in order to survive another day—outside a shabby grocery, shivering in a threadbare coat. You who are so quintessentially French, I see you doubly threatened because you are French and a Jew. I realize the value of a community that does not sanction such actions. We are all the offshoots of a tree—France—and I will bear witness to your truth as you would to mine. For us French exiles, the aim must be to reactivate the stored seed, frozen by the German occupation. We must help you. We must free you in the land where you have a basic right to put down your roots. You are forty million hostages. It is always in the deepest recesses of oppression that new truths are born; forty million hostages are seeking their own new truth. We yield in advance to that truth.

It is you who will teach us. It is not for us to carry the spiritual torch to those who imbue it with their substance. Perhaps you will never read our books. Perhaps you will never listen to our speeches. Perhaps you will despise our ideas. We who are not involved in the founding of France, we can only serve her. Whatever we do, we will have no right to any gratitude. There is no possible comparison between fighting in freedom and being crushed in the night. There is no possible comparison between the profession of a soldier and that of a hostage. You are the saints.

Diary of Léon Werth[3]

February 22, 1943

After the war the problems of Europe and the world will have to be solved. Each one of us is—to an infinitesimal degree—responsible for our civilization. What is my hope at this present moment? The terrace of the inn at Fleurville—the Saône seems to stretch away endlessly, without any banks, mingling with the horizon and a fringe of pale trees. We ordered fried fish and creamed chicken. Will we ever see the inn at Fleurville again, Tonio? Will we regain our civilization?

In March, at about the time Saint-Exupéry received his embarkation papers for North Africa, Reynal and Hitchcock in New York published his most famous work, The Little Prince, *in English and French.*

Dedication of *The Little Prince* to Léon Werth

TO LEON WERTH

I ask the indulgence of the children who may read this book for dedicating it to a grown-up. I have a serious reason: he is the best friend I have in the world. I have another reason: this grown-up understands everything, even books about children. I have a third reason: he lives in France where he is hungry and cold. He needs cheering up. If all these reasons are not enough, I will dedicate the book to the child from whom this grown-up grew. All grown-ups were once children—although few of them remember it. And so I correct my dedication:

TO LEON WERTH

WHEN HE WAS A LITTLE BOY

Letter to his Wife, Consuelo[4]

[mid-April 1943]

You see, Consuelo, I'm forty-two years old. I've had many accidents. I can't even jump with a parachute. Every second or third day my liver gives me trouble, every second day I'm seasick. Ever since my accident in Guatemala, I have a continual humming in one ear—and material worries without end. Sleepless nights spent working away at a task that all my worries make more difficult to accomplish than moving a mountain. I feel so tired, so very tired.

And I'm off, I who have every reason to stay, who have innumerable reasons to reform, I who have already waged a tough war. I'm off. . . . I have firm commitments on that. I'm off to the war. I cannot bear to be far from those who are hungry. I know only one way of being at peace with my conscience and that is to suffer as much as possible—to seek the greatest possible suffering. That will certainly be granted to me—a man unable, without physical pain, to carry a five-pound package, get out of bed, or pick up a handkerchief from the floor. . . . I'm not going off to die. I'm going off to suffer and in that way be close to my people. . . . I don't wish to die, but I'm ready—gladly—to go to sleep like this.

Antoine

Saint-Exupéry sailed for Oran with a troop convoy on April 20. He described this voyage, which lasted until May 4, at the beginning of his "Letter to an American" of May 30, 1944 (see that date).

Also on board was Dr. Henry Elkin, a Jungian psychoanalyst from New York.

Recollections of Henry Elkin[5]

Saint-Exupéry and I were fellow passengers on a troopship that sailed in convoy from New York, as I vaguely recall, on or shortly after April 20, 1943, and arrived in Oran on May 3. I was being transferred from the New York headquarters of the Office of War Information to its office in Algiers. We were among a small number of army officers and civilians, all except Saint-Exupéry in military uniform, quartered in individual cabins on the spacious deck. Below us, in obscurity, was a teeming hive of troops in the vast hold. Since I alone spoke French and Saint-Exupéry was inexhaustibly communicative, we were always together during the trip. I was so bound up in his aura that I've never recalled any of our fellow passengers: They were but shadows or faceless puppets that peopled our surroundings. Meeting Saint-Exupéry on this ship turned out, in fact, to have been a most critically important encounter, setting my life on a path that decisively influenced its future course. For after two months or so in Algiers I resigned to enlist in the U.S. Army, a move I doubtless would not have made had not Saint-Exupéry, on hearing me say on shipboard that I felt a tinge of shame for working in propaganda, immediately rejoined with, "Quit and join the army." The fateful quality of my encounter with Saint-Exupéry is for me somehow reflected, although I can't say that I believe in astrology, in the fact that we have the same birthday.

While still tied up in New York harbor, Saint-Exupéry showed me the single copy of *The Little Prince* which his publisher had hurriedly run off the press to give him before sailing, prior to its official printing and distribution. It must have been when I opened the book, read a few lines, and looked at the drawings under his playfully intent and expectant gaze—one of his facial expressions that penetrated and forever marked the image of my own soul—that my fateful bond was sealed. On the following days he often read to me, making alterations, from the manuscript that later appeared as *The Wisdom of the Sands*. Apart from our conversations, ranging from the playful to the ultra-serious, and simply being in his ruminative or quiet presence, I recall from the trip only visiting, with and without Saint-Exupéry, the engine room and the densely packed underworld of the ship's hold, seeing other ships in the convoy herded by lean destroyers, hearing intermittently the muffled explosions of depth bombs, and, during a dark night, slowly gliding through the straits, overshadowed by the Rock of Gibraltar, before landing in Oran.

Only now do I grasp the revelation that Saint-Exupéry was for me: that marvelous unity—an embodiment of moral and psychic integrity—of thought, feeling, and action which reflects the original childlike, or rather infantile, purity of the human soul. Tending toward states of deep regression, not "in the service of the ego," as prevailing Freudian theory would have it, but to achieve communion (co-union) between the Primordial Self and the cosmic, Primordial Non-Self or Other—the latent reference of Freud's concept, "Father." This momentous course leads to that precarious, ultimate disjunction between the experience of inner and outer reality, the realms of originary human imagination and of spatial-temporal physicality, from which religion, psychosis, and human creativity all have their primal source. Given its infantile springs, the integrity of creative genius— attested to by numerous examples—is gravely threatened by the social and cultural fragmentation of modern times. In 1943 Saint-Exupéry, rooted in his deep communal love of France, anguished sorely over the collective passions, inherently cruel and vicious, that estranged his countrymen from one another. Throughout our voyage, his stream of thought always culminated in the appeasing prospect, once the war was over, of entering the monastery of Solesmes. Our conversations, mainly his speaking and my listening, often ended by his intoning a liturgical chant. For in anticipatory imagination, he was already leading a monk's life. In my memory of him, a tall, loose-limbed, ruminating or playfully smiling figure with the solid, earthbound gait of a bear, only the Benedictine robe is missing. As Saint-Exupéry's life and World War II both turned out, this final culmination of his spirit did not prove to be prophetic. But given current trends, may not its prophetic import be still to come?

Summary of Events

Boufarik: May and June 1943, training on a Simoun aircraft.

Laghouat: same period, training on a Bloch 174 and a North American aircraft.

Morocco: on a mission May 1943. Visit to Dr. Comte in Casablanca.

Oujda: June 4 to July 1, 1943, with Group 2/33. Training on a P-38 Lightning with Colonel Elliott Roosevelt's 3rd Photo Group (whose adjutant was Colonel Karl L. Polifka).

Tunis (La Marsa): July 2 to August 18, 1943; July 21, first flying mission over southern France in a P-38; August 1, landing incident; August 11, last flight.

Algiers: summer 1943, at Dr. Pélissier's.

Casablanca (Anfa): stay with Dr. Comte, summer 1943.

Algiers: autumn–winter 1943–4, at Dr. Pélissier's.

Naples: Group 2/33 stationed there from January to May 1944. Saint-Exupéry was there April 23 and 24.

Villacidro: May 1944, with Group "Morocco" of the 31st Medium Bomber Squadron.

Alghero: May 16 to July 16, 1944, with Group 2/33.

Castellane–Saint-Raphaël: engagement of July 31, 1944.

On May 5, 1943, Saint-Exupéry went to see General René Chambe, who had become Minister of Information to General Henri Giraud.* Chambe recalled the following remark by Saint-Exupéry: "I've kept my appointment, though six months late, for which the Gaullists are to blame."

---

* Commander in Chief of French forces in North Africa.

General Chambe allowed Saint-Exupéry to rejoin Group 2/33
at Laghouat, under the command of René Gavoille, who had been
promoted to group captain. Chambe also arranged for Saint-Exupéry
to meet General Giraud.[6]

(Unsent) Letter to an Air Force Officer
Who Had Recently Joined the Gaullists[7]

[1943?]

My dear X,

I've just reread your note. It seemed infinitely friendly and sincere. Then I heard of a long conversation of yours about me. It was a painful attack. Not painful as such—I'm completely indifferent to the opinion of others—but because it came from you. I admit that I write few letters, but once formed my attachments are as hardy as trees and always grow. I've no recollection of having given up our friendship. . . . What I think of a man doesn't derive from what he thinks of me. If I were to proceed in such a manner I would despise myself. But I'm disconcerted when—because of life's incoherence—such an accident happens to me. I need to believe, not in you in particular, but in mankind.

You have joined active Gaullism; that is your perfect right. It may be your duty, according to your way of thinking. Each of us has a duty to fight for the religion in his heart. I'm no royalist, but I have great respect for the royalist gentleman of the old school. I may be tormented by certain aspects of your dogma without giving up any of my esteem for you. One loses nothing of the quality of one's inner substance if one takes over certain ideas out of pure motives. But nothing is gained by espousing certain ideas out of vile motives. And ideas are worth as much as the men who propound them are worth. But their very diversity is a boon. That is the breeding ground of future syntheses. My friend may very well be someone whose ideas run counter to mine and who thereby enriches me. He forces me to overcome what we are. Friendship is born from an identity of spiritual goals—from common navigation toward a star. Then we strive toward the same meeting place. But the chosen star— for example, the greatness of France—does not give the course to follow. The choice of means is a question of reason. And reason can err—in fact, mostly errs. It is by trial and error that the truth is reached in physics—by trial and contradiction. You know this. If you argue against me, I shall respect your share of error because of your share of truth, which is no doubt as convincing as mine. I don't mind in the least that you should be exploring other paths. It gives us a better chance of finding the right one. My friendship rests on the common choice of a star.

I like it when a physicist is enthusiastic about his solution. I like it when you turn historian or sociologist and become enthusiastic for yours. This passion is not sectarian bigotry. Bigotry only sets in when you monopolize truth; when you become "totalitarian"; when—despite the fact that no formula is satisfactory and each final synthesis is only an ideal direction, not an attainable goal—you lock yourself up in your own formula in order to condemn all others; when, like the Academy of Medicine in Pasteur's time, you condemn Pasteur to death; when you condemn Galileo or Einstein. It's only in police matters that the opposite of truth is error, and truth the opposite of error. And I don't see you setting up police methods as your ideal. Civilization rests on spiritual communion, embracing a diversity of thinking, of ways and means, and of adduced theories. In my book my friend looks and observes as I do— but thinks differently from me. To think here means to verbalize, to hinge one syllogism to another and make up a theory.

Your ideal is the defense of spiritual values. You are anti-

Nazi, antitotalitarian. You refuse to guillotine Lavoisier.* Between the exiled Aeschylus and his judges, you choose Aeschylus. You laugh at a Hitler who forbids the reading of Einstein. You don't require Pascal to express an opinion on the domestic policies of his time, and you enjoy reading Montaigne—and then at the first opportunity you betray your views on humanity. You turn your living truth into a dead Koran. And in the name of your dead dogma, you demand that Lavoisier, Aeschylus, Einstein, Pascal, and Montaigne embrace it on pain of death. You will no doubt invoke the urgency of the moment—"There is no time for . . ."—as if there had ever been "time for . . . ," as if all urgencies weren't imperatives at the time. Naturally, you'll say that your policy is not political but national, but what policy does not seek to condition man's as well as the nation's fate? As if you could live an isolated day of the history of humanity! In fact when the problem of spiritual values, of the respect for spiritual values, crops up—as it has so often in the course of history—when you are at last faced with it, you at once betray it.

Leave rudimentary doctrines to policemen. You, surely, move on a higher plane! What sad times are these that enlist Lavoisier, Aeschylus, Einstein, Pascal, and Montaigne in the political-propaganda corps—whatever the policy, even if it should be a desirable one. At your level it is a question of establishing respect for knowledge, respect for human dignity, for love of justice and country. You are on a level not with court-martial judges but with apostles—a spiritual apostle whose coming is slow.

If you join this or that group, I shall certainly not reproach you for it, on condition that you prove to be its most noble component, like the fruit of the tree—on condition that your joining it ennobles it. Each of us possesses different organs for

---

* Antoine-Laurent de Lavoisier (1743–94), one of the founders of modern chemistry; executed during the French Revolution.

different functions. It is better to be either the brain or the heart.

Of me you've said, "Saint-Exupéry is a cad not to have joined Gaullism in America. We shall demand an explanation from him. What has he been doing these last two years?"

Sectarian bigotry always leads one astray. I knew you as an honest pilot who refused to resign his commission after the armistice. You didn't think you'd acted wrongly. And even if today you consider that you were wrong at that time, I don't think your mea culpa should go so far as a charge of self-betrayal. You said, "I acknowledge that my reasoning was wrong, but I've never swerved from my principles. Yesterday, too, I was honorable." You knew yesterday that you were a pledge for the honor of others (not all others, but show me a group where all are honorable!). You betray them a little in betraying yourself. You were not a Gaullist yesterday—or rather you were one only to the same degree that all Frenchmen at home or abroad were Gaullist. But that did not conflict with your role as a French officer opposed to the occupation of North Africa, ready to risk your life against Germany. In taking off for Gibraltar, you would have felt that you were betraying all that was best in your comrades. And I, in what way was I wrong in not betraying you?—me, a sectarian sitting and enjoying the American horn of plenty, how was I wrong in refusing to call you a villain?

Saint-Exupéry wrote to Sylvia Hamilton[8] from Algiers: "If I was not a Gaullist in New York, it was because their policy of hatred was not the right course for me. I was reproached for the kind of life I led in New York, I was insulted. So today I'm happy to be able to testify to the purity of my intentions by risking my life. One can sign only with one's own blood. . . ." In the same letter he wrote that he hated Algiers, "this muggy city. It's an impure climate—a sort of dumping ground of humanity."

Group 2/33 was attached to the American 3rd Photo Group under the command of Elliott Roosevelt, based at Oujda. The P-38

Lightning in service there was a fighter adapted for use as a strategic reconnaissance aircraft; several cameras—able to take hundreds of pictures on a mission—replaced the guns. It was a fast long-range aircraft, capable of flying at great heights. Regulations called for pilots to be no more than thirty years of age. Thanks to special intervention by General Chambe with Eisenhower's headquarters,[9] Saint-Exupéry received permission to fly.

On May 30, General de Gaulle arrived in Algiers. On June 3, the French Committee for National Liberation was founded, jointly presided over by Generals Giraud and de Gaulle.

Letter to Curtice Hitchcock[10]

[Oujda, June 8, 1943]

Dear Curtice,

I requested and was allowed to join my comrades of Group 2/33, with which I flew before, and which still exists.

One of the squadrons of the Group has been seconded to the American Army Air Force and is serving under its orders. [censored passage] I'm part of that squadron. I'm a pilot on a plane called [censored]. It is, I believe, the fastest plane available at present. In fact it is a fighter plane, but we use it for reconnaissance work.

You see, I was not too old, since even with the Americans I was able to remain a pilot. I refused any other job when I came to Algiers. (They wanted me for propaganda work again.)

Dear Curtice, I've done everything I could to remain with my fellow flyers, away from politics, cities, and offices. I'm leading the routine life of an American base and . . . I'm learning English! I hope to stick it out as long as possible, though I can feel that I'm no longer twenty years old (but I haven't told anyone!).

I'm very impressed by your compatriots. They are efficient, healthy, and remarkably well trained. Relations between my comrades and them are very friendly. Yours is a great country.

As to your war effort, it is not properly understood when seen from America. Seen from here, it is stupendous. You cannot imagine the effect such an avalanche of equipment produces.

What I most admire is a certain courage, simple and noble at once. A "cheerful courage." I don't express myself well, but I'll write about it all later on. Dear Curtice, I love your country very much.

Curtice, I've been right, I think, in my ideas about my country's affairs these last two years. I don't like de Gaulle any better now. There's a threat of dictatorship there—national socialism. I dislike dictatorship, political hatred, and the dogma of the one-party system. While national socialism is dying elsewhere, there really seems no point in reinventing it for France. I'm all too impressed by these madmen. Their taste for massacre among Frenchmen, their hoped-for postwar policy (a European bloc) will lead to France, weakened as much as Spain, becoming nothing more than a satellite of Russia or Germany. Truth, for me, does not lie in that direction.

One day you'll share my opinion, Curtice. You'll smile sadly, remembering how I was called a fascist because of my refusal to espouse Gaullism. Does anyone still think that Gaullism represents democracy and General Giraud tyranny? Rather would I reproach Giraud for having been sheeplike in giving in on every point to the dictator-elect. What do they think in the United States, Curtice?

Best love to you all. I know nothing of *The Little Prince* (not even whether it has come out!). I know nothing at all. Please write to me.

I think it would be better if you wrote to me c/o a friend in Algiers who will forward my mail to wherever I am: Dr. Georges Pélissier, 17 rue Denfert-Rochereau.

How I would like to see you all again!

Yours,
Saint-Ex

Letter to Georges Pélissier[11]

Dear Dr. Pélissier,

I'm sending you this short note since I don't know when I'll be back. I would so much like to get a letter from you giving me all the world news. Here I live in a complete desert—in a camp—three to a room (for me this proximity is the greatest of all sacrifices). At mealtimes, we line up with our mess tins, get our share, and eat it standing up. I feel a bit outside of life, like being underneath the great hall of Saint-Lazare railway station. You know I don't wish for anything else. I have stubbornly done what I thought right, whatever X may think.

In fact, my dear friend, I'm not at all well and that is depressing, because my physical condition makes everything difficult—as difficult as a climb in the Himalayas—and this added sacrifice is unfair. Little things become unnecessary tortures. Just coming and going in the hot sun in this large camp tires me so that sometimes I feel like leaning against a tree and weeping with rage.

But I so much prefer these ills to the ghastly atmosphere of polemics. All I want is peace—even eternal peace. . . .

I don't want to discuss myself and my problems endlessly. I can't stand explaining anymore—I don't owe anybody anything and those who don't know me are foreign to me. I'm too tired, too weary to change. I have enough enemies to instruct me—I need friends in whose friendship I can rest as in a garden.

I'm at the end of my tether tonight. It's depressing: I should like to love life somewhat, but I can't. While flying the other day, I thought I was done for, and I regretted nothing. . . .

Affectionately,
Saint-Ex

Letter to Georges Pélissier[12]

Oujda, June 1943

Dear friend,

My address is:

> Captain de Saint-Exupéry
> 3rd Photo Group
> APO 520
> U.S. Army

Letters take about three days. Telegrams? In case of need, ask to phone me via Major Gelée. (Ask for Central Security—then ask for General Giraud's headquarters—then ask for Major Gelée.)

I've piloted the racing machine (670). It's all right, but I'm not very well physically.

Don't forward my letters, but let me know what letters I've received.

Do forgive this chore, but I'm unlikely to receive many letters.

Dear Dr. Pélissier, my old friend, I'm endlessly sad.

Yours ever,
Saint-Ex

Unmailed Letter Addressed to General X
[General Chambe?][13]

[Oujda, June 1943]

Dear General,

I've made several flights in the P-38. It's a fine machine. I wish I'd been given that present in my twenties. At forty-three, I realize sadly that after logging more than 6,500 flying hours the world over, I no longer find great pleasure in such games. A plane nowadays is a mere means of transport—an instrument of war in this case—and if I submit to the speed and altitude, at an advanced age for this profession, I do it so as not to refuse any of the burdens of my generation rather than because I hope to recapture the satisfaction of bygone times. That's sad, perhaps—but perhaps not. No doubt I was wrong when I was twenty. In October 1940, coming back from North Africa, where Group 2/33 had been sent, my worn-out car had to be overhauled in a dusty garage and I discovered the value of a horse-drawn cart, and with it the grass bordering the road, the sheep, the olive trees. Those olive trees were no longer just so many trees along the road, whizzing past at 130 kilometers an hour. I now saw them in their natural rhythm, slowly making olives. The sheep no longer merely served to reduce one's speed, they came alive. They ate and gave wool and the grass once again had a meaning, since they grazed on it.

I felt I was coming back to life in the only place on earth where the dust is scented. (I'm being unjust; the same is true in Greece and Provence, too.) And I felt that all my life I'd been an idiot. . . .

I'm saying all this to let you know that this gregarious life in an American base, these meals gulped down standing, these comings and goings between one-seater planes with 2,600 horsepower and a sort of abstract construction where we sleep three to a room—this terrible human desert, in short, does not make my heart rejoice. All this, like the 1939 missions with no hope of success or return, is like a sickness to be overcome. I'll be "sick" for an uncertain time. But I feel I have no right to avoid contracting this illness. That's all.

And so I'm profoundly sad. I'm sad for my generation, which lacks all human substance. Having known no spiritual values beyond the bistro, mathematics, and the Bugatti, this generation finds itself assembled for a herd action, devoid of color. But this goes unnoticed. Consider the military phenomenon a hundred years ago. Consider how much effort was put into satisfying people's spiritual, poetic, or merely human aspirations. Today, when we are more dried out than any brick, we smile at this naïveté—the costumes, banners, songs, music, victories (there are no victories nowadays, nothing that conveys the poetic impact of Austerlitz; there remain only phenomena to be absorbed, slowly or quickly). All lyricism sounds ridiculous. People refuse to be awakened to any kind of spiritual life. They carry on (conscientiously) a kind of conveyor-belt activity. As young Americans put it, "We conscientiously accept this thankless job." And propaganda the world over makes futile, desperate efforts. The sickness does not lie in any absence of individual talent, but in the way people are forbidden, under pain of ridicule, to turn to the great refreshing myths. In its decadence, humanity has descended from Greek tragedy to the plays of M. Louis Verneuil.* (You can sink no lower.) This is the century of advertising, of the Bedaux system,† of dictatorships, of armies with neither trumpets nor banners, nor masses for the dead. I hate this age with all my might. In it humanity is dying of thirst.

There is one problem and only one in the world: to revive in people some sense of spiritual meaning—some spiritual uneasiness—of immersing them in something like a Gregorian chant. If I had faith, I know that once this "thankless, necessary job" is over I could not bear to do anything but withdraw to the monastery of Solesmes. We can no longer survive on refrigerators, politics, card games, and crossword puzzles. We can no longer live without poetry, color, love. One only need listen to fifteenth-century village songs to realize how much ground has been lost. Nothing remains but the robot-voice of the propaganda

---

* Louis Verneuil (1893–1952), fashionable French playwright who lived from 1940 to 1945 in the United States.

† A time-study method used to determine wage rates; named after the French-American industrial engineer C. E. Bedaux.

machine (forgive me). Two billion human beings hear only the robot, understand only the robot—become robots. All the upheavals of the last thirty years have only two causes: the dead end of the nineteenth-century's economic system, and spiritual despair. Why did Mermoz follow his fool of a colonel, if not from spiritual hunger? Why Russia, why Spain? Men tried out the Cartesian values but, except for the natural sciences, without success. There is only one problem: to rediscover that there is a spiritual life, which ranks higher than intelligence and which alone satisfies man. This goes beyond the problem of religion, which is only one form of spiritual life (but perhaps one leads to the other). Spiritual life begins when a human being is "seen" to be more than the sum of his component parts. The love for one's own home—this love that is impossible to feel in America—is part of the spiritual life, like the village fête and the cult of the dead. (I mention this, because two or three paratroopers have been killed since I got here. But they were neatly conjured away: They were no longer of use. This is due to the attitude of the age, not because of America. Humanity no longer has any significance.) One absolutely must speak to humanity.

Of what use is it to win the war, if we are faced with a hundred years of revolutionary convulsions? Once the German problem has been dealt with, the real problems will become apparent. At the end of the war, it is unlikely that speculation on the American stock exchange will be enough to divert the attention of the world from its true problems, as it did in 1919. In the absence of a strong spiritual current, sects will spring up like mushrooms and devour each other. Marxism itself is showing signs of aging; it is splitting up into a multitude of contradictory neo-Marxist movements. Unless of course a French Caesar confines us in a neosocialist concentration camp for eternity. . . .

Ah, General, what an odd evening. What a strange climate. From my window I look out and see the windows of those faceless buildings lighting up. I hear the different radios emitting their vapid music to an idle crowd from overseas, incapable even of feeling nostalgia. One might mistake this resigned acceptance for the spirit of sacrifice or moral grandeur. That would be a great mistake. The bonds of affection that men feel for mankind or for things are so lacking in tenderness and solidity that absence is no longer felt as it used to be. Like that terrible Jewish story: "You're going out there? How far away you'll be!" "Far away from where?" The "where" that was left behind was no more than a bundle of old habits. In this age of divorce, one divorces oneself just as easily from things. Refrigerators are interchangeable—and homes, too, if they represent nothing more than a bundle of habits—so also with a wife, a religion, or a political party. One cannot even be unfaithful: There is nothing to be unfaithful to. Far from where? Unfaithful to what? A human desert. How quiet and sensible the men in my group are. I can't help thinking of the old Breton sailors, going ashore at Puntas Arenas, or the Foreign Legion let loose on a town—of the ferocious and intolerable longings that always arise when males are too closely penned up. It always took strong policemen, strong principles, or strong beliefs to hold them. But not a single one of them would have dreamed of being disrespectful to a goose-girl. Nowadays, men are kept quiet by gin rummy or bridge, according to their social position. We are astonishingly emasculated. And so, we are finally free. Our arms and legs having been cut off, we're left free to walk. I hate this age, where, under a universal totalitarianism, people become as docile as cattle—polite and quiet. And that's supposed to represent moral progress! What I hate about Marxism is the totalitarianism it leads to. It defines people as producers and consumers. The main problem is that of distribution—as on the model farms. What I hate about Nazism is the totalitarianism that it affirms. They make the workers of the Ruhr pass by a Van Gogh, a Cézanne, and a color print. The workers naturally pick the color print—that is the people's truth! One safely locks up the Cézannes and Van Goghs in a concentration camp and then offers color prints to the submissive cattle. But where is the United States heading, and where are we heading, for that matter, in this age of universal bureaucracy? Robot-man alternating between work on the conveyor belt and gin rummy—stripped of all creative power, incapable of creating, from the depths of the village, a new dance or a new song, spoon-fed with a ready-made, standardized culture as one feeds hay to cattle. That is what man is today.

And I remember that, barely three hundred years ago, a lost love could lead someone to write *The Princess of Cleves* or withdraw to a convent for life—so ardently was love felt then. Today also people commit suicide, but their suffering is on the order of a violent toothache. It has nothing to do with love.

True, there's the first step to be considered. I can't bear to feed generations of French children to the German Moloch. Our very substance is threatened. When it has been saved, then the fundamental problem of our time will have to be considered— the meaning and purpose of humanity. No answer is forthcoming and I have the feeling of moving toward the blackest times in the history of the world.

I don't care if I'm killed in the war. But what will remain of what I have loved? By that I mean not just people but customs, certain indispensable intonations, a certain spiritual radiance. What will remain of the farmhouse lunch under the olive trees of Provence, or of Handel? The things that endure, damn it. What is valuable is a certain ordering of things. Civilization is an invisible tie, because it has to do not with things but with the invisible ties that join one thing to another in a particular way. We shall have perfect musical instruments (mass-produced), but where shall we find the musician?

I don't care if I'm killed in the war, or in a fit of rage at these flying torpedoes that have nothing to do with flying and turn the pilot amid all his buttons and dials into a sort of accountant. (Flying is also an ordering of ties.) But if I return alive from this "necessary, thankless job," there will be only one problem for me: What can and what should we say to people?

I understand less and less why I'm telling you all this. No doubt in order to tell someone, because this is not something I have a right to say. One must promote peace in others and not complicate matters. At present it's good for us to be mere accountants in our fighter planes.

Since I began writing, two comrades have gone to sleep next to me in my room. I'll have to go to bed too, since I presume my light disturbs them (I do miss having a corner of my own!). Both men are wonderful in their way—upright, honorable, clean, loyal. I don't know why, looking at them sleeping, I feel a sort of impotent pity; because although they are unaware of their unease, I feel it. Yes, they are upright, honorable, clean, loyal, but also terribly poor—they are so much in need of a god.

Dear General, forgive me if this poor electric bulb which I'm turning off now has prevented you from sleeping too. And be assured of my friendship.

Saint-Exupéry

René Chambe recorded other pessimistic remarks by Saint-Exupéry about the dangers that seemed to threaten the world:[14]

"Perhaps the universe won't recover for a million years. It will languish in complete decay amid its rubble and ruins. Why do we fight? Because we cling desperately to principles we cannot bear to see disappear. It's pretty childish. Those principles—for whom and for what? But we have no choice, we cannot do anything else. When one has written the books that you and I have written, we cannot fail to put them into practice. What would be said were we to act differently? What would we ourselves say? We are struggling in a maze of tests. This is our test.

"You see, General, I hate this age. When this war is over, nothing but emptiness will be left. For centuries, humanity has been descending an immense staircase whose top is hidden in the clouds and whose lowest steps are lost in a dark abyss. We could have ascended this staircase; instead we chose to descend it. Spiritual decay is terrible.

"I don't care if I'm killed in the war. If I survive, what sort of 'job' could I seek refuge in? There are no jobs among the ashes."

On June 14 Saint-Exupéry arrived in Algiers, preceding Group 2/33, which was on its way to the Algiers airport (Maison-Blanche). On June 16 he met Robert D. Murphy,[15] President Roosevelt's special envoy to North Africa. On June 17 Saint-Exupéry sent Murphy a letter recapitulating a request he had made in the name of his comrades.

Letter to Robert D. Murphy[16]

[June 17, 1943]

Dear friend,

I feel that I didn't express myself very clearly yesterday and was a poor advocate in putting my ideas to you. I don't hesitate to renew my request as I have our mutual interest in mind and not any personal advantage.

If I begin with some introductory words about myself, it is in order to state the case clearly, not to put myself forward. But I think that under the circumstances I can be of some service to my country.

You probably know that my books *Night Flight* (Prix Fémina, 1931) and *Wind, Sand and Stars* (Grand Prix du roman de l'Académie Française, 1939) were the top best sellers of the last ten years in France. Perhaps you know that, as it happens, the same is true in your country. *Wind, Sand and Stars* was a best seller, a Book of the Month Club choice, and a National Book Award winner in 1939. *Flight to Arras* was at the top of the best-seller list for months. This good fortune—whether deserved or not—gives me a particularly large double audience. I tell you this for a reason that means a lot to me.

As you know, I took part in the 1939–40 campaign as a flyer in one of the squadrons that worked hardest and suffered most (Reconnaissance Group 2/33). I stayed with them up to the last minute. But I refused to join the Gaullists in America. It seemed to me that a Frenchman abroad should be his country's advocate rather than a witness for the prosecution.

I accepted it with equanimity when I was called a "fascist" by the one-party faction and only broke my silence to write *Flight to Arras*, and later a long article in the *New York Times* on the necessity of reconciliation among Frenchmen at the time of the events in North Africa.

I then immediately asked to rejoin my fighting unit and I believe I was the first French civilian to join the ranks in North Africa. Since I still prefer a silent fighting post to any other job, I am at present a flight captain on a P-38 in Colonel Roosevelt's photo group.

Rightly or wrongly, I continue to believe that the salvation of my country lies neither in ruthless purges carried out by the one-party fanatics nor in the strange ideology of a European bloc in which France—linked to eighty million Germans and a hundred and sixty million Slavs—would be no more than an impotent satellite. Just as I refused to criticize the State Department's policy on maintaining representation in France, in the name of salvation for North Africa, so I refuse in the name of my country to join any campaign against a future Franco-Anglo-American alliance. Rightly or wrongly, I believe this is our only chance for salvation.

But you must help me.

By a lucky chance, eight of the pilots in my group work

with the pilots of Colonel Roosevelt's group. I'll write a new *Flight to Arras*, and in it I'll defend the views that are important to me. But in order for my book to achieve its aim, we must take part in your missions as soon as possible. There are things that I have a right to say if my comrades and I have returned from a flight over Italy or France. I will only be listened to if my comrades and I have risked our lives for our ideas. If I don't take part in the war, I can only revert to silence.

I know how very complex you consider the problem of rearming the French Air Force (it seems to me, by the way, that you're wrong), but in any case your scruples do not apply where we are concerned, since we represent an experienced unit used to working together. Please use your influence with Colonel Roosevelt. This is urgent, because decisions will soon be made that may ruin our chances. May I ask you to request Colonel Roosevelt to dine with you, Major Challes, Major Piéchon (in charge of my group), and myself? I don't feel I'm being indiscreet. After all, our larger aims coincide. However insignificant you may consider what I have to offer, at least admit that it is something positive. Since any other decision would carry no definite advantage, let me plead in favor of the two points I care about:

a) The transfer of my group as a whole, not just half of it. It would be sad to split up such a splendid unit. We therefore request that the whole group be attached to Colonel Roosevelt's group and equipped with P-38s. We represent a hard core of trained pilots and mechanics. What would be the use of splitting up the small number of P-38s you are prepared to give the French?

b) That the already trained pilots be sent on military missions.

There have been rumors about the strain of high-altitude flights on the older pilots among us. There is no truth in this, and I wish to dispel any remaining doubt. We are all recent veterans of high-altitude flights.

Forgive this letter, my dear friend, I'm not foolish enough to imagine that the addition of our twenty pilots will make any great difference to the balance of forces in the field, but I do believe (forgive my presumption) that something useful can come out of the fraternity of our joint war effort.

> With sincere thanks,
> Your friend,
> Antoine de Saint-Exupéry
> c/o Dr. Pélissier
> 17 rue Denfert-Rochereau
> Tel. 39442, Algiers

On June 19 Saint-Exupéry was declared fit to fly at high altitudes. It was noted, however, that "slight pain was apparent from an old fracture when a pressure equivalent to an altitude of 35,000 feet was maintained." On June 25 he was promoted to Major.

On June 28 his fellow flyer Jules Hochedé was lost at sea during a training flight. The funeral took place on July 1.

On July 2 the squadron moved to the airfield of La Marsa, near Tunis. Saint-Exupéry spent several happy weeks staying with René Gavoille and working on The Wisdom of the Sands. *On July 21 he completed his first mission over southern France.*

(Unmailed) Letter to Lieutenant Diomède Catroux[17]

[Tunis, summer 1943]

My dear Catroux,

. . . I feel a vague unease at living through these nights outside time . . . amid this parasitic vegetation. These people give the impression of mushrooms living on a tree they know nothing of and naïvely pursuing their cruel little existence. I'm thinking in particular of a pseudo-civilian [yesterday]* who in place of charm had a sort of ready-made poise—a Ritz-like poise that I hate. With his gift for malingering and for baccarat, such a man is as alien to me as a gudgeon in an aquarium. If I don't consider advocating a "purge" where he's concerned, it is because he seems to me already dead. If this species reappears after the Liberation, it will be because France is rotten to the core—but it isn't. I cannot become interested in such an individual, even in order to kill him.

You're one of the rare sane people that I've met in this country—at least among those who think. But you find any number of decent people among those whose intelligence has not warped their instincts. What is difficult is to preserve the instincts while thinking. A certain kind of French bourgeois is ghastly, but the pure doctrinaires of Marxism are just as ghastly. (Read *Il est minuit dans le siècle* by my Russian friend Serge.) As for the intellectuals at the University of Paris at the time of the trial of Joan of Arc, they were even more so. Read their deliberations! I don't give a damn; it's a kind of ransom. The blacksmith loses his muscles when he becomes a geometer. If the ignominy of Joan of Arc's trial (which is one of the great documents that I know of) had resulted in a purge of the Sorbonne, then in effect Descartes, Pascal, and Bernoulli would also have been purged—since the Sorbonne was a necessary link in the chain that produced them. Someone who devotes his life to algebraic simplification no longer understands the growth process of a leek, which is complex. Someone who devotes himself to growing leeks is ill-equipped to study nebulae. The opposite of error is not truth, but above all the opposite of truth is not error. As long as man has not become a god, truth will be expressed through contradictions. And from contradiction to contradiction he reaches truth.

* Crossed out in the original.

For fundamental reasons I hate the myth of the purges. Not because I want to save some Tom, Dick, or Harry I'm indifferent to—he'll die, anyway. But when a class, a caste, or a group vanishes, and its evil vanishes with it, the invisible good that was part of it also disappears. Yesterday we spoke of the grocer-Frenchman, dear to Louis Philippe's heart. Perhaps we ought to search further back. The aristocracy of the eighteenth century, had it merged with the masses after an English type of revolution, might have inspired them with its idea of grandeur and its rituals of courtesy. Its extravagance might have become generosity in a simple lamplighter. But it was cut off root and branch because of its vices—and with it a part of the heritage of France.

France needs a common measure in order to draw together her different qualities, her different theses around a transcendental image. One cannot formulate this problem without drawing a distinction between intelligence and spirit. Spirit indicates the direction, the spiritual point of view—the choice of star. For example, I will fight for the dignity of man. Intelligence—guided but not instructed by this compass—hesitates as to the choice of means to be employed according to the dictates of reason. And reason is fallible—in fact, it is always wrong, since no logical truth is completely valid either in space or time. Two physicists contend in the name of the same religion of knowledge. Lieutenant Catroux and I fight in the name of the same French greatness. And that is enough to make me feel fraternal toward him, even if he chooses means different from my own. A Frenchman who makes France's salvation dependent on the survival of two-year-old children, even if it means taking a step back in some respects, cannot, to my way of thinking, be considered the spiritual enemy of another Frenchman who makes France's salvation dependent on purity of principle and, in the name of that absolute, is prepared to accept the sacrifice of all the children. The truth is contradictory; and both parts of the truth had to be saved. Man's field of vision is minute, and each person only considered his part of the truth. Action demands these simplifications—that is only human.

But when that stage is past, when France has been saved, body and soul, then I shall divide men not according to the means they chose, or the necessary functions they assumed, or their thinking, but on their choice of star—on the spiritual ideal that dominated their thinking. My brothers are those who have loved as I have, not reasoned as I have—and I use the word "love" in its initial sense of "spiritual contemplation."

I'm not expressing myself clearly, although I know precisely what I'm trying to say. I know very well which men I can bear and which I can't. And it's been like a breath of fresh air meeting a few men like you in this sordid North Africa.

Do phone to organize a real dinner with Comte. Thanks.

St-Ex

In July 1943 the French squadron received congratulations on the missions it had flown in P-38 aircraft.[18]

Letter of Congratulation from the Commanding Officer, Troop Carrier Command, Northwest African Air Forces (NAAF)

1. As of June 18, 1943, all the photographic missions requested by the troop carrier units of this base have been fulfilled.

2. All the personnel of Photo Unit 4 contributed greatly to the difficult task of meeting all the demands of the troop carrier units. In every case, the work accomplished by this unit has been more than satisfactory.

3. The General Headquarters of NAAF Troop Carrier Command wishes to congratulate the Commanding Officer of Photo Unit 4 for the excellent work accomplished and to express

the hope that this unit will again work with the troop transport units in the near future.

By order of Brigadier General Williams

Signed: S. J. W. Timberlake

1st Lt. Air Corps

Actg. Asst. Adjt. Gen.

1st Transmission Ref. R.G.I.

S.F.—520 U.S. Army

July 15, 1943

To the Commanding General of the French Air Force
c/o NAAF General Command, APO U.S. Army

1. We read with pleasure the congratulations transmitted by the Commanding General of NAAF Troop Carrier Command and I wish to congratulate especially the men in Reconnaissance Group 2/33 of the French Air Force for their share in the success of Unit 4.

2. It is requested that this letter of congratulation be reproduced and a copy thereof delivered to Captain de Saint-Exupéry, Antoine.

Signed: Elliott Roosevelt

On August 1 Saint-Exupéry left on his second mission. He had engine trouble, overshot the field on landing, and slightly scraped a wing.

On August 12, using this incident as a pretext, the Americans reminded Saint-Exupéry that the absolute age limit for flying a P-38 was thirty-five. General Carl Spaatz put him in the reserve command.

On August 17 the conquest of Sicily was completed.

On August 19 Saint-Exupéry left Tunis for Algiers.

Letter to X[19]

[Algiers, August–September 1943]
. . . I'm almost at the end of my tether. I always have the impression that I shall suffer greatly. The present time reminds me of Aéropostale on a gigantic scale. . . . The war missions were my peace. I was indifferent to the intrigues of others while I felt within myself the peace of such a clean death. But when unemployed I feel miserable and vulnerable—without civic identity. And I understand absolutely nothing of life.

Above all, I hate polemics; I can't stand them. They are the worst torture on earth for me. It may be strange, but that's how it is. And I cannot bear prison. Beyond that I can stand anything—even being at 35,000 feet, exhausted as I am today, even wounds or being fried alive. . . .

It's difficult to fight for "nothing." I don't like the Gaullist bandwagon because of certain of its aspects. But it is a bandwagon. There is nothing opposing it—just a ridiculous, dust-covered old dummy. Where can I go for a breath of fresh air?

The only thing that remained were the war missions—a few hours spent flying over France—something of the dignity of an icy scaffold. It suited me fine. But being unemployed I have nothing to look forward to that means anything to me. Sickening discussions, polemics, slander—I'm bored by the morass I'm entering. Oh, God, how men disgust me. Life among them seems no more than a concentration camp to me. . . .

Everything is mediocre, I can't stand it. At 35,000 feet I was beyond mediocrity. Now I no longer have that outlet.

Back in Algiers, where he was staying as always with Dr. Pél-issier, Saint-Exupéry was irked by his forced inactivity. To help pass the time, he devised mathematical problems like the following.[20]

The Pharaoh's Problem

A pharaoh decided to erect a massive stone monument in the shape of a parallelepiped rectangle, built exclusively with cubic stones cut to the size of 10 centimeters per surface, and whose height was equal to the diagonal at the base.

He ordered each of a certain number of civil servants to collect together an equal part of the exact number of stones needed. Then he died.

Contemporary archeologists found only one of the piles of assembled stones. They counted 348,960,150 stone cubes.

They knew nothing of the other piles of collected stones, except that the total number of assembled stones was—for mystical reasons—a prime number.

This discovery enabled them to calculate the precise size of the planned monument, and to show that there was only one possible solution.

Now do the same yourself.

N.B.—(a) As this problem does not require any elaborate numerical manipulation, we supply you with the breakdown of 348,960,150 into primary factors:

$$2 \cdot 3^5 \cdot 5^2 \cdot 7 \cdot 11 \cdot 373$$

(b) Any solution arrived at by a laborious empirical method does not count.

Solution to the Problem

I. The necessary and sufficient condition for the validity of the formula $a^2 + b^2 = c^2$ for *whole numbers* is that the numbers a, b, c should be of the form:

$$a = 2\,pmn$$
$$b = p\,(m^2 - n^2)$$
$$c = p\,(m^2 + n^2)$$

(p, m, and n being whole numbers)

This theorem Saint-Exupéry had established in advance.

II. We know that:

$$a, b, c = 348{,}960{,}150 \times x \quad (1) \ = kx$$
$$a^2 + b^2 = c^2 \quad\quad\quad (2)$$
$$a, b, c$$

are whole numbers   (3)

x is a prime

number   (4)

III. We have:

$$a, b, c = 2\, p^3 mn\, (m^2 + n^2)\, (m^2 - n^2) = kx$$

from which we immediately deduce that $x = 2$ since x is a prime number.

IV. We know that:

$$k = 348{,}960{,}150 = 2 \cdot 3^5 \cdot 5^2 \cdot 7 \cdot 11 \cdot 373$$

The object is to identify $2, 3^5, 5^2, 7, 11, 373$ with the expression

$$p^3 mn\, (m + n)\, (m - n)\, (m^2 + n^2)$$

We establish that p^3 can only be 3^3, then we write out the following table:

$2 \cdot 3^2 \cdot 5^2 \cdot 7 \cdot 11 \cdot 373$	18	25	7	11	373
	9	50	7	11	373
	9	25	14	11	373
	9	25	7	22	373
	9	25	7	11	746

We must find $m, n, m + n$, and $m - n$, which is only obtained by:

$$11 + 7 = 18 \quad\quad 25 - 19 = 7 \quad\quad \text{(line 1)}$$

Finally we have:

$$p = 3$$
$$m = 18 \quad\quad\quad - 2 \cdot 3^2$$
$$n = 7$$

Therefore:

$$m + n = 25$$
$$m - n = 11$$
$$m^2 + n^2 = 373$$

V. Finally:

$$a = 6 \cdot 18 \cdot 7 = 75^m 6$$
$$b = 3 (18^2 - 7^2) = 82^m 5$$
$$c = 3 (18^2 + 7^2) = 111^m 9$$

On September 8 came the announcement of the capitulation of Italy, which had in fact occurred on the 3rd. Montgomery landed in Calabria on the 3rd, Clark at Salerno on the 9th. Naples was taken on October 1. Giraud sent French troops to liberate Corsica (September 13 to October 5). During this time a German rescue party freed Mussolini from arrest, and the fighting front stabilized along the line of the Garigliano River.

On November 5, 1943 Saint-Exupéry fell down the stairs at Dr. Georges Pélissier's, where he was staying.

(Unmailed) Letter to X*

> One does not die for ideas,
> One dies for the substance—
> One dies for the essential Being.

Dear X,

You have reawakened in me an old drama and made me absolutely wretched. You know me well enough (in fact, you're the only one who knows me among that crowd that yaps about me) to realize that far from feeling the serene peace you attributed to me in the heat of the discussion, I have spent the last two years torn by an inner anguish that I wouldn't wish you to experience. Not being an exhibitionist, I've hardly mentioned it to anyone. This silence may have created an illusion.

---

* Unpublished rough draft annotated by the author; addressed to a friend who reproached him for his reservations about some aspects of Gaullism.

Each of us has his own way of being. Some achieve complete peace of mind once they are involved in action. Then there are no more problems. I was completely happy flying for Aéropostale until your friend Serre—through his disastrous good intentions—destroyed the spirit of sacrifice that reigned there; just as I was happy in 1939–40 in a simple fighting job or, until recently, flying in a P-38 Lightning. I don't care about my skin, and the atmosphere in which I lay it on the line appeals to me spiritually much more than any other. Or perhaps I should say "sentimentally" rather than spiritually, but there are times when the spiritual and the sentimental clash within me. If this had not been the case I'd be an anarchist. I met the same atmosphere as that of Aéropostale among the anarchists in Barcelona during the Spanish Civil War. The same gifts, risks, and fraternity, and the same high conception of humanity. They could have said, "You think as we do," but if they had said, "Then why aren't you one of us?" I would have had no answer to give that they could have understood. They lived according to sentiments, and where sentiments were concerned I had no objection to raise. In the same way, I've no objection to Communists, or Mermoz, or anyone, anywhere, who risks his life and prefers, above all other things, the daily bread shared among comrades. While I have faith in man born of Communism, I have little faith in the Catalan anarchist as a guiding element in this emergence of man. The anarchist owes his greatness to the fact that he didn't triumph. If he had succeeded, nothing but a vain, formless mass, without interest to me, would be left. (I'm ready to explain why.) Why should I destroy my spiritual goal, merely in order to taste a certain sentimental ecstasy? It would be cowardly. The spiritual must prevail over the sentimental. Put very simply, this is what you accept when you punish your son. Therefore, in certain cases, I cannot establish my peace of mind by fighting for anarchism and against injustice, profiteering, and all the other

errors of mankind. Stalin's people—the anarchists' worst enemies—were also fighting against the errors of mankind. And
so were Franco's people, and Déroulède's, and Maurras's, and
Saint-Just's, and the Pope's.

Your problem was simple, since it was purely emotional. I
love because I love, and I hate because I hate. The causes are
sufficient. Being what I am, my problem was more difficult to
resolve. I can well imagine that you risked your life in France
in the Resistance. It was your duty and I would have done the
same. But abroad, I felt I was saddled, against my will, with an
overwhelming responsibility. Not overwhelming in its power—
I would have been a mere drop in the ocean—but in its object.
And without any risk to myself. (Or rather without that risk
having any meaning. I don't care about risk. I do not invest risk
with the power to absolve me. I know full well how much
greater are some forms of courage than courage in the face of
death. How easy that is—even more so when one is in a
rage.)

Personally, I was against the armistice. I stole a plane in
Bordeaux. I recruited forty young pilots on the street, crammed
them into a four-engine Farman, and flew them to North Africa
to continue the war there. It was a failure because the armistice
applied to North Africa as well. So I was unemployed.

But from that time onwards I was worth what my word
was worth. The objective I was going to be responsible for—to
a small extent—was the survival of the French people. You can't
reinvent history. You can enumerate the disasters of the past,
but you can't prove or disprove to me the hypothetical disasters
or advantages of an imaginary train of events. But anyone who
had the power—to however small an extent—of adhering to or
breaking the armistice agreement (this was in fact the heart of
the matter) could only weigh this very seriously.

1. In 1940 all adult males of military age on French soil

would go off to rot in the German camps—legally. Six million prisoners instead of two million.

2. North Africa would be occupied by Germany. I know that tunnel thinking insists on denying this. (There was even a rumor that Germany was too exhausted by the French campaign to be capable of a further effort!) I consider that a Germany with its power still intact (not yet sapped by the enormous American war machine and overwhelming Russian power, or by the ten million German dead) would have crushed North Africa either via Spain or via Sicily in two weeks. (Would Franco have resisted?) Here there would have been 200,000 unarmed men. Even supposing that a vast quantity of tanks, planes, and modern machine guns, as opposed to our muskets, would not have greatly changed the proportion of losses, Germany still had only to sacrifice 199,999 prisoners, wounded, or dead, in order to find herself facing one solitary soldier—probably the commanding general, who is unarmed in any case. (And I leave aside the Arab problem.)

3. German blackmail would be complete. Survival of the French towns would depend solely on the railway moving stock, and this moving stock on axle grease, and the axle grease on oil supplies in Hamburg or Rumania. The officers at Wiesbaden* were faced with this blackmail every day.

4. I cannot forget that in Warsaw alone three million Poles† were sent to the gas chambers. I do not think that the threats against France contained in *Mein Kampf* were any less dangerous than those directed at Poland.

5. At a time when Belgium had already furnished Germany with two million workers, France had so far exported only a

---

* After the armistice of June 1940, a French-German Armistice Commission was convened at Wiesbaden.

† Needless to say, an erroneous number. As can be seen in paragraph 7, Saint-Exupéry also had little knowledge of the persecution of Jews in France.

hundred and twenty thousand. In this way another two million prisoners would have been added to the already existing two million legal prisoners.

6. And what about the threat of population transfers?

7. And the Jews? You can hate Peyrouton* for conceding what he did. Nevertheless he was a bulwark for you. The two hundred thousand French Jews would never have survived a German domination as yet undiminished in its pride. As it is, Léon Werth lived, came and went, even wrote.

8. And the problem of America's presence? (I'll come back to this.)

Vichy was without doubt terrible. But an organism creates its own anal passage for evacuating excrement. Men who work in sewers are not fond of sweet smells. Jailers rarely have compassionate souls. He who asks the victor for axle grease is less disgusted by the smell of dung. All of this concerns functions. (As for the police—like all police forces nowadays, they are revolting.)

My problem in France would probably have been killing Pucheu.† My problem in America was quite different.

It was a sad thing, when I left France just before the armistice. I remember a road that I was driving along at night, in the rain. It was a black night. I had switched on my headlights. When I was stopped by a traffic jam, I suddenly became engulfed in a sort of popular riot. Soldiers besieged my car and threatened to kill me. Why? My headlights. In this morass of rain and mud, under a cloud cover of three hundred and fifty feet, I was bringing down upon them the celestial fury of Hitler's bombers. As one of these heroes shone his flashlight at me, they started insulting my insignia of rank. I was the embodiment of war

---

* Marcel Peyrouton, onetime Minister of the Interior of the Vichy Government.

† Pierre Pucheu, also an ex-Minister of the Interior. He was subsequently tried, convicted, and executed.

among arms dealers and capitalists. I felt an unutterable disgust and almost a need to be massacred by this rabble. You can imagine the thick, insulting voices and the smell of sweating fear. I felt the abject terror all around me—the faces, the voices, the attitudes, all were despicable. I felt deeply ashamed.

As for the civilians! We were billeted in eleven different villages during the retreat. What a reception we got, we who were dying! Not a single voice was raised in favor of resistance. Not a whiff of patriotic spirit—degraded cattle—total egotism—the severing of all ties.

Where was the France I thought would awake someday? That image of the French people hating the regime that condemned them to shame—oh, . . . what a lie! The Germans were received with a ghastly sigh of relief by this herd of cattle.

Of course there were many exceptions—ourselves, for a start. Between spells of wallowing in this filth we got ourselves killed, without a word, on war missions. There was Mandel,* a peasant here, a soldier there; but basically it was not the government that brought about the armistice, it was France. That was obvious. Not merely the French capitalists or military authorities, not Jean Prouvost,† not Pétain, but France as a whole—with them. And to console myself—I was against the armistice—I told myself that this overpowering wave, this resignation of fear, perhaps had some kind of significance. It is wrong of me to look at this too close up. Everything is ugly when seen at close range: My sweetheart seen through a microscope is merely an expanse of gritty surface. Everything is equally ugly in a short time span. A snapshot of Pasteur . . . blowing his nose, or making some gesture . . . is of no use. One must study man and peoples from a distance—in space as well as time. Man seen at close

---

* Georges Mandel, Minister of the Interior under Paul Reynaud in 1940. He opposed the armistice and was killed by the collaborationist militia in 1944.

† Industrialist and newspaper magnate.

quarters consists of offal. The essence is missing. But the race was badly run. The war was fought without arms. We were cracking up. We would have lost two million men just in order to postpone the German advance for twenty hours. Some innate instinct in the species refuses to allow such a useless hemorrhage. Two million dead, six million taken prisoner, three or four million deported, and, looming over all, the specter of population transfers. . . . And for the rest: women, children, and old men begging for axle grease from the invader in order to try to survive. You know what pressing need is. The noble nation nevertheless turns to black-marketeering. You yourself told me the same about Russia. The French people have cried out ever since they saw the German wave gathering momentum for solidarity or help in building a rampart against it. Yet they have been called disturbers of world order and then left to fight Stukas and tanks with millstones. To whom should they give thanks? To what godhead do they owe the fact that their very substance has been cast into a deep pit from which it will not rearise?

It is part of my line of conduct to wish to continue the fight. In the same way, when Germany was saved in 1918 by an armistice and avoided enemy occupation, the people suffered for a time under Stresemann's pederasts, but the armistice ensured the survival of the conditions necessary for its recovery, its toughening, its pride. When Germany signed, it was certainly the duty of any German Déroulède* to denounce the iniquity of the armistice. Germany gave in before all was destroyed. Germany gave in before the death blow was delivered. But was the hidden conscience of the nation killed when it refused to continue a war that had come to mean sterile and irremediable loss of substance? How many pages have been written in France on this premature armistice that saved Germany? Of course it man-

* Paul Déroulède (1846–1914), poet and politician, president of the League of Patriots, author of *Chants du soldat.*

ifested itself in an apparent refusal to fight, a material acquisitiveness whether sordid or not, anarchy, egotism, and a cringing baseness toward the victors (worse than in France!). (The armistice was more of a celebration there than it was here!) It is true that this armistice of ours also contains its share of ugliness and exalts ugliness. . . . He who dies is braver than he who capitulates. To conquer or to die—a tall order. . . . But that is anthropomorphic reasoning. Something that has meaning for an individual may not be valid for a whole people. In the same way, what is valid for a cellular organism may not apply for a complex individual. There is grandeur in an individual being killed defending a rampart—that constitutes a sacrifice. But where is there any grandeur in a whole people's suicide? You yourself don't want it. You'll condemn any individual who in any way serves the enemy out of fear of death. But you won't condemn the workmen at Billancourt for not committing collective suicide, hundreds of thousands of them in one day, rather than keep the German machines going. You would even consider this gesture gratuitous, as it would only result in the bombardment of the Renault works by the RAF, while leaving the machines running. This is no paradox. Let some die for the common good—that is a duty. For all to die is absurd. If you dedicate yourself to France, you will die for it. You will die for something greater than yourself, but you will not kill the thing that has become your religion in order to save it. The workers at Billancourt considering collective hara-kiri don't know for whom they are to make this sacrifice, and so they drop the idea. The workers continue to run the machines, even while hoping that they will be destroyed and the workers themselves decimated, because then those who died would be dying for others.

So true is this that in the polemics that took place in New York it had to be decided for whom the French sacrifice should be made. I don't mean "the share of sacrifice accepted by France" but "the complete annihilation of France." It was to be made for a vaster entity: the Allied side. "Let all French children die, rather than England be defeated," said Vogel.* One pert childless female said to me: "If I had children in France, I should be proud to hear they were starving." But when the children die, France dies—in whose name? That of others. But this is an émigré's pastime. It's a phrase as easily said as "Pass me the mustard" or "It's hot." The concept "Allied side" is a provisional one. Your Gaullism is preparing to fight America or even England. . . . The people think more slowly and more "authentically." The new divinity lacked the substance that would have inspired it in its sacrifice. The entity to be saved was France— already ruined and threatened with disintegration because of your divisions. That entity was no longer perceived. The vaster "Allied" entity was impossible to recognize.

My thesis in all this rhetorical jousting is that a people is embodied in neither the French Chamber of Deputies nor the American Senate nor the Fascist Council, but in the value of its substance. But Tréfouël,† Pascal, a silent mother watching over her sick child, the readiness to help or accept sacrifice in a certain workers' community on strike, any gratuitous kindness independent of ideas—these things override ideas and outlast political changes, just as the oak outlasts the changes of the seasons. Heritage is not transmitted by means of the politician's formulas.

There can be no sacrifice for a policy. There can be sacrifice only for an entity and its substance or some part of its substance. I may sacrifice myself for the freedom of my brethren, for the freedom of the individual, for the liberty of Greece or Italy. I will not sacrifice the freedom of my nation for that liberty. We are the conquerors of a vaster entity. I might sacrifice my nation

---

* Lucien Vogel, director of several women's magazines.

† Jacques Tréfouël, chemist and bacteriologist who contributed important work on sulfonamides and later became head of the Institut Pasteur.

to the apotheosis of humanity. But then I would look for the virtue of man not in political formulas but only in his intrinsic substance. A crusade that saps the lifeblood of a people can only be dedicated to God. . . .

It's time to think straight and to invest with meaning words that have lost all market value, because the problems we face are novel, confused, and contradictory—like honor and dishonor. . . .

Letter to Dr. Henri Comte in Casablanca[21]

> [Algiers, November 14, 1943]
> c/o Dr. Pélissier
> 17 rue Denfert-Rochereau
> Algiers
> (Please use air mail, or it takes six months.)

Dear old friend,

A most ridiculous thing happened to me. As I was walking in the hall of a completely darkened house, I failed to see six marble steps, elegant no doubt when lit up in bygone times. I suddenly found myself suspended in midair—but not for long. I heard a tremendous crash—it was me.

I found myself lying on my back, delicately supported at two points by the solid angles of the mock-marble slabs. These two points were the coccys (?) (you'll correct the spelling) and the fifth vertebra in the lumbar region. Despite such a small ledge inflicting such a big shock, the steps were intact.

As for me, I can walk more or less. The X rays were inconclusive. For curiosity's sake rather than treatment (things seem to be improving by themselves), I should like to find out whether, according to you, the small bump on this vertebra is due to my fall. I enclose a partial X ray of my future skeleton.

Apart from all this, I'm sad. I regret Casablanca, Marrakesh, and the oasis of Dar Limoun, as well as sweet little Rouliote.

That virtuous shepherdess moved with such exquisite grace among the bulls of Leclerc's army.

Here gradually, bit by bit, we return to the golden age. Cot,* Le Troquer,† Queuille,‡ and Mendès-France§ have been divested of their mothballs—they may still come in handy. It is touchingly turn-of-the-century.

Next year there will be a lot of shooting, which will be somewhat melancholy. What will be the use of this bloody harvest? The real problems are not being faced. Power is used to impose a creed. Where is the creed? Whatever the genius of General de Gaulle (and I do rather believe in his political genius), he will one day have to direct the passions he has aroused. He will have to give form to something. I know what he feels, but truth is found not in sentiments but in the mind. What will he bring forth?

His speeches more or less satisfy my sentiments. But then who is not in agreement where sentiments are concerned? Greatness of the nation, influence of the best among us, social justice . . . who would disagree with that? Or with law and order, culture, and contentment? I agree with the aims, but the important factor is the means used to achieve them. From what sort of philosophy do the words "law and order," "justice," "culture," and "contentment" derive? What will they really mean? Unless they are thought out, they will remain meaningless. And if they are thought out, they must be sharply defined. Every concept is an empty one unless its meaning derives from a

---

* Pierre Cot, jurist, deputy for Savoy; Air Force Minister 1933–37. Member of the Provisional Consultative Assembly in Algiers 1944–45.

† André Le Troquer, Commissioner for War and the Air Force.

‡ Henri Queuille, medical doctor, deputy for Corrèze. Several times a cabinet minister. He joined General de Gaulle in London. Member of the Provisional Consultative Assembly in Algiers.

§Pierre Mendès-France, lawyer, deputy for the Eure, fought in the Gaullist Air Force. Minister of National Economy in the Provisional Government of Algiers. Later Prime Minister and (1954–55) President of France.

specific, real structure. Law and order, justice, culture, contentment are all very well, but according to which creed? Marx, *Mein Kampf*, or the Holy Scriptures? There should not be too much shooting before it has been decided whom to shoot.

Islam cut off heads according to the Koran, the French Revolution guillotined according to Diderot, Russia executed according to Marx, Christianity had itself decapitated (which comes to the same thing) according to the Epistles of Saint Paul. The exalted emotions that justified these massacres were only means that nature put at the disposal of the mind. Will emotions for the first time in man's history kill for their own sake, without knowing in which direction they're heading? To my way of thinking, passion is a blind monster—even if the passion is a noble one, even if it is pure.

Joseph Kessel,* returning from France via London, told me three days ago: What we need is a bloodbath. It's inevitable, it has always been like that. And then a conciliator like Henri IV must come along.

That is where he goes wrong. The passions aroused during the religious wars were only the consequence of intellectual debates. It was Calvin versus the rabble, not one drunken trooper against another. When the Spirit is aroused—each time it is aroused—it sheds blood, without knowing it or troubling about it. The bloodshed takes place on a lower level. Neither Diderot, nor St. Paul, nor Calvin, nor Marx, nor the rabble, nor Confucius thought of bloodshed. But in the last analysis the Spirit walks on human feet. Then it is blind and it devastates. It turns into emotion on the lower level, and then there is shooting. Whether it is better or worse that this should be so is immaterial. There is no choice. That is how things are. But there is a higher level too: a head above the shoulders, a mind above the heart. So I

---

* Writer and aviator of Russian origin, member of the French Academy. In 1942 he was captain of a squadron in England.

should know what seed I am sowing—but, as it is, I know nothing.

The most recent bible is a hundred years old: Marx's *Capital*. This bible is much too old to be worth a lot of bloodshed. In any case, Marxism is not the issue. General de Gaulle, if he wants to build something, must spend sleepless nights. For the first time in human history, there is no bible. Will he be able to prevent his disciples from building at random, like schoolchildren? The trouble is they'll be cutting into irreplaceable material.

I'm very worried about the future.

But friendship remains, and you know I'm fond of you.

Saint-Ex

Letter to X[22]

[Algiers, late 1943 (mid-November?)]

. . . I'm lying motionless. . . . Six steps in the dark hall. . . . I was supposed to dine with Schneider and some friends, but I forgot the steps and found myself in midair—though not for long. I fell full length on my back, coming to rest with my coccyx on the edge of one marble step and my fifth lumbar vertebra on another. Two rather hard points of support, but too little to absorb my inertia. The coccyx held firm, but not the vertebra.

Naturally, the shock to the spine went to my head and I remained stunned for five minutes lying on the steps. Then I took stock. I said to myself that the spine could not possibly have withstood such a shock. It must be fractured. So I tried to move my legs; they moved. So the broken vertebra must be one without spinal marrow—an inedible one, as it were! It was true. I'm not that stupid. The fifth lumbar vertebra has no marrow.

Then I got up. I could just stand up. I walked with very small steps toward my tram and went to my dinner party. The pain confirmed my diagnosis. I said, "I'm sorry to be late, but I've fractured a vertebra." Everyone laughed, including me, and nobody took any further interest in my vertebra.

On returning home, I pushed a note under Pélissier's door: "I fractured a vertebra in a fall on your steps, just before going out to dinner. Please take a look at it tomorrow morning." I had a bad night and couldn't get to sleep until 8 A.M. He read my note and went off to the hospital. He had no time, so Séverine said.

I was puzzled. I had a rather official lunch date and only my own diagnosis as an excuse. So I went to my lunch very, very slowly. On returning at 4 P.M., I felt poorly; he was having office hours, so I had Séverine ask him to examine me. He felt the vertebra and said something like: "You see, it doesn't move!" I answered, "It's broken all the same!" He laughed.

I sounded very pretentious. So I said humbly, "What should I do about the pain here?" He explained the problem very, very clearly and then advised some form of exercise.

As I seemed a little hesitant, he assured me that he had known any number of people who had been knocked about, even hit by trains, without suffering broken vertebrae. How heavy a train must be! By comparison six steps seem like child's play.

So I went out to another dinner, even more slowly; I urged myself on, saying, "This will be the right exercise"—but I was not really convinced.

The next day the Soviets were holding a big reception in the pretty garden of a palace—very elegant, though with nothing to drink but orangeade.

All the ministers, generals, and Christians in Algiers were strolling on the lawn. They were waiting for the lions. They whispered: "Where are they?" They were in fact standing right there, but looked like respectable bankers. And they handed around the orangeade. This very much reassured the Christians.

But I was left in the lurch, standing on that lawn without a chair and unable to take a step. When an acquaintance passed, I asked, "Have you got a car? No, well at least keep me company for a few minutes! Standing here all by myself I look like a perfect fool"—which was true.

Still, I tried to put up a good front, meanwhile inching my way toward the exit. I managed it quite discreetly, and Admiral Auboyneau finally took me home.

When I tackled Pélissier again about my injury, he said, "But bad bruises hurt a lot! If you really want reassurance, go and see this radiologist, who is very good." I did want reassurance, so I went to see the radiologist, who said after a quick look at the X rays:

"But you're crazy to be walking around! You have a transverse fracture of the fifth lumbar vertebra, coupled with a slight vertical indenture and oozing from the bone. Moreover, the whole vertebra has been displaced several millimeters to the left!"

"I see."

"A fractured vertebra is no laughing matter. It'll mean three months in bed or you'll be crippled for life!"

"I see."

"Surely you can feel that you have a fractured vertebra?"

"Oh, yes!"

I then returned to Dr. Pélissier's house. I felt like a cracked jar. I walked with infinite care. I said to Pélissier:

"It's fractured. You'll have the X rays tomorrow."

"How do you know it's fractured?"

"The radiologist said so."

"What an idiot. These wretched radiologists who try to diagnose. Let them stick to their photography!"

"Dinner is served." This was said by Séverine.

"Where shall I have it?"

I felt fragile, tired, and in pain, and I would have liked to lie down. But I realized immediately that Séverine was old and the radiologist an idiot, so I sat down on a chair.

Next day the X rays were delivered. Pélissier spent five minutes agreeing with the radiologist's conclusions. Then he recovered himself.

"It's hereditary!"

"Oh, why?"

"Because."

"I see."

I felt ridiculous at the precautions I took, but I was in more and more pain.

"All the same . . . Such a violent shock . . ."

Dr. Pélissier became irritated. I had understood nothing whatever.

"But I've seen people who've fallen from the fifth floor without so much as a scratch!"

That is the present state of affairs. I sent a friend to see the radiologist, who confirmed his diagnosis of a fractured vertebra. And I'm in pain, that's for sure. And the vertebra is a marrowless one. In any case it will grow together again—perhaps too much.

II

I'll continue with my letter. This is the second act. Being unable to move, I had to tell the military authorities.

They came and took the X rays with them. They said it was a fracture. Out of courtesy I asked Pélissier to come and meet them. He said, "This radiologist is a pretentious fool. You should have new X rays made at the hospital."

He very kindly took me to the hospital and said to the army radiologist (a rival of the previous one), "Dr. B. is being silly. A fracture would look like this."

The army radiologist made some more X rays, which were unsuccessful, then tried again with better results. One could see the morning mists of a Japanese landscape. It was very pretty.

Through the morning mist one could see something that might have been a hill or a vertebra. The army radiologist said, "I'm not of the same opinion as Dr. B."

Then he reflected why. Pointing to the spot which had been declared congenital two days before, he said: "This is only the projection of the sacrum."

"Indeed!" said Pélissier.

Since it couldn't be a fracture, it had to be something else—in my case a congenital projection.

On our way home, Pélissier said, "You see, I didn't put any words in his mouth."

"Oh, no."

And so the army also rejected my fracture, and I went back to walking around in order to get better. I'm not cured yet.

III

Today it is seven days since I fell down. I'm neither better nor worse. But Pélissier tells me that severe contusions can last up to three months, at least the pain can. At any rate, I'm very tired.

Pélissier sensed that I was still not convinced, so he brought back an X ray of a real fracture.

"This is what a true fracture looks like."

And I must say that I would myself have diagnosed it. In place of a vertebra there was a zigzag and all around it a myriad of little pieces, each the size of a tooth. I said, "That really does look like a fracture."

I thought: If it wasn't a train or a five-story building, it must have been a torpedo—in view of the damage, at least a torpedo.

And I added timidly, "Is that all that was left of the man?"

"What?"

"Is this vertebra all that was left?"

Then he took back the X ray.

. . .

And now I'm of two minds. Perhaps my horned vertebra is not poisonous. But I'm uneasy because I have an odd pain. I'd prefer to know the reason; I'd rather it turned out to be a simple fracture. And I feel oddly guilty walking around. And since there is nothing wrong with me, I feel even guiltier staying in bed. So?

I need to be settled in a destiny. It's as if I were sitting in a train that is permanently immobilized at a signal. I'm neither at war nor at my own work, neither sick nor well, neither understood nor shot, neither happy nor unhappy—but desperate.

Desperation is a curious thing.

I need to be born. I realize that I would have welcomed it if they had kept me stretched on a wooden plank for years—a spiritual destiny. In the same way, I would have liked to have been allowed to continue flying war missions in a P-38 Lightning—a soldier's destiny. I would equally like to be hopelessly in love—destiny of the heart.

To love without hope is not despair. It merely means that one is reunited only in the infinite—and along the way the pilot star is unfailing. One can give and give and give. It's strange that I can't believe, that I don't have faith. One loves God without hope: That would be something that would suit me —the monastery of Solesmes and Gregorian chant.

Gregorian chant—high seas. I've often reflected on that. Before leaving Lyons in 1940, I went up to Fourvières on a Sunday afternoon. It was, I think, the hour of vespers. It was cold and the church was empty except for the choir. And I felt as if I were in a ship. In the choir, the crew; and I a passenger— a secret passenger. I felt as if I had crept in there by stealth— and I was dazzled. Dazzled by an obviousness I was never able to hold on to.

· · ·

I feel great pity for people because they are asleep to something, but I don't know what it is. . . .

. . .

Why am I going to have such pain? You don't know how afraid I am—and I don't mean my vertebra. That was worth it. . . . The shock was great (the shock in the head) and that clarified my ideas. It's strange—it has clarified my nerves, too. I was very tense, so much so that I couldn't write more than two consecutive pages without my hand tensing up. I became quite illegible. . . . In my letters during the last months my writing changed even on the second page. . . . Well, the shock of my fall changed all that. It straightened out something that had been tangled up. It's strange. . . .

. . .

Here is another note for Mama. God knows how sad all this is. How can one find oneself again? Of course one can't. And where can one find oneself—in home, customs, beliefs? That is so difficult today, and it makes everything so bitter.

I try to work, but it's hard. This frightful North Africa rots the heart. I'm at the end of my tether—it's like a tomb. How simple it was to fly war missions in a P-38 Lightning. Those stupid Americans, when they decided that I was too old to fly, built a wall around me. D. can do nothing—how should he be able to? I'm afraid for my work, even practically speaking.

I'm ready for anything. . . . As far as I'm concerned, I'm completely without hope. I feel a little sorry for myself. I feel sorry for everyone. When I hear certain judgments passed on myself, I hate all judgments passed on others. It's just that people are desperate; they're deprived of sunlight. Let's say that what I value in someone is the opportunity to lift him up. I can give anyone more than I can receive. I am so alone. Let's say that what I value in someone is the chance to raise a drowning face above the surface of the water, to hear a certain sound in his voice or see a certain smile on his face.

Let us say that I am only drawn to imprisoned souls.

If for three seconds you manage to win the trust of someone who is lost and bewildered, you will be amazed at the change in his face. Perhaps I have a vocation as a dowser. I will look deep into the earth. Those who are perfect have little need of me.

I'm told, "A drowning man sinks far deeper than you think." So I hurry. It's not madness. I alone know what I'm going to bring up to the surface. How strange that I should have taken so long to understand this. But it's true that I never had the gift of "being" happiness or of receiving it. If I "am" happiness it frightens me, as if I had indicated a wrong path. As for receiving—I have so little to receive. I may seem cruel if I fail to console a sorrow or gratify a desire—cruel toward the heart and body, but not the soul. I've never been cruel. I belong a little to those who use me as a guide—wherever they come from. The vocabulary I use to express myself is purely religious. I came to realize that in rereading "Caïd."* It's hard to explain, but it's not accidental: "a vehicle, a path, a carriage for the leader of leaders?" I understand nothing beyond this. I don't understand how anyone can "deserve" me. I'm no reward. Nor do I "deserve" anything. I deserve nothing. And I can't think otherwise than I do.

In fact I'm fed up with myself—with my difficulty in expressing myself in words about anything. I'm imprisoned in myself—even symbolically. What can I do against landslides? I'm utterly discouraged. I want desperately to write, but the climate here is profoundly unhealthy for me. My life is draining away. I've never felt so worn, and all to no purpose. It's horrible. Oh, for those straightforward P-38 missions only two months

* From *The Wisdom of the Sands.*

ago! Those stupid Americans didn't know what they were doing when they deprived me of those flights. . . .

Letter to his Wife, Consuelo[23]

[Algiers, undated]

New York, the divisions, the disputes, the slanders, and now the affair with A.B.*—all these things have finally put me off completely. They are tiresome. Surely that is not what being a man means—it's false algebra. And all of them are a little like that. That's not my country. I'm willing to be shot down in order to protect the peace of Agay,† or Lazareff's dinners, or your ducks (which by the way you cook the wrong way—the skin isn't crisp), in order to protect certain "qualities." The quality of the things I love—loyalty, simplicity, games of chess with Rougemont (he's a good fellow), fidelity, dedicated work; not a game with truth in which everyone tells lies in exile, far from everything human.

Letter to X[25]

[December; received February 18, 1944]

It's three in the morning. . . . I can't stand it any longer. Why am I so desperately, desperately sad? There's no news of any great interest. My vertebra was indeed fractured. Pélissier admitted it a month later, grudgingly, on the evidence of an indisputable X ray. In the meantime I had been walking around, as I had no moral right to lie abed. (P. would have taken that as an insult.) It was a little like a Chinese torture. Luckily, in the case of this kind of fracture, walking about didn't make

---

* An allusion to a controversy with the poet André Breton and his friends. Breton had criticized *Flight to Arras* severely. In reply Saint-Exupéry wrote an "open letter" to Breton, but he neither finished it, nor sent it, nor published it.[24]

† Home of Saint-Exupéry's sister, Gabrielle d'Agay.

much difference. (I've consulted others about this.) At the moment I'm still in pain; I'm in a bad way by evening, but I manage. My morale is not good at all.

I cannot stand this age. . . . Everything has got worse. The mind gropes in darkness and the heart is frozen. Everything is mediocre, everything is ugly. I reproach them for one thing above all: They don't inspire joy, they don't bring out talent, they don't draw anything out of people. All they have introduced is something like a sinister proctor in a second-rate school.

They are like a sickness inside me. . . . It's strange. Never in all my life have I felt so alone. It's like an inconsolable grief.

. . .

I don't know whether I can be cured of this. There is no one to treat me.

What human squalor there is in this country—the trash-heap of continents! This sideline of history, where everything deteriorates. This musty, parochial, backward atmosphere—and the ridiculous figurehead at the helm. If you could only see their "Assembly"* you would weep. And what trouble they take to prevent the ridiculousness of it all from provoking general laughter. It's so comic as to be frightening. And the pretentious attitudes they adopt while awaiting permission to begin the shootings. I believe they lack any sense of humor. So many monstrous injustices have already been committed.

All this follows from the power of stupidity.

Utterly stupid.

Totally ugly.

I've had enough.

The impossibility of communicating in this day and age is what hits me hardest. I have such an urge to leave all these

---

* The Provisional Consultative Assembly of the French Committee of National Liberation.

idiots. What is there left for me to do on this planet? They don't want me? All the better—I don't want them. How I'd love to throw in the towel as a contemporary. I cannot find a single one who is able to tell me anything that interests me. So they hate me? It's merely tiring and I'd like to rest. I should like to be a gardener tending his vegetable patch—or dead.

. . .

I have sometimes been happy in my life—but not for long. Why can I no longer feel happy even for one morning? The most depressing fact is that I have nothing to hope for.

My sadness is not physical. I know that I can't stand social anguish. I'm full to bursting with that noise, like a seashell. I don't know how to be happy on my own. With Aéropostale, life was joyful—how grand that was! I can no longer stand this misery.

. . .

Life in a cell, without faith. This ridiculous room.* This complete absence of any tomorrow. I can't tolerate this abyss any longer.

. . .

Some news, not much.
I met General R. (ex-Secret Service).
"Hello, Saint-Ex! By the way, watch out."
"Why?"
"Watch out, left and right."
"What do you mean?"
"We ought to warn each other, among friends."

---

* Dr. Pélissier had put at Saint-Exupéry's disposal a small room furnished with wardrobes on one side of the window and with a small bed along the remaining stretch of wall.

"Thanks."

That's all I could get out of him.

Then at the Interallié I ran into Laugier*—that miserable worm, rector of the Academy. He is one of the bigwigs of the regime. He sees me:

"Hello!"

"Hello!"

And then, very loud, in front of the other pundits: "Hello, dear member of Pétain's National Council."

"Me?"

"Yes, of course. Pétain is admirable!"

And one of the pundits dining with him said: "You are a member of the National Council?"

Laugier: "Of course, naturally!"

You remember that sinister appointment,† proposed by some pig! You remember my fury and how I refused immediately. What's the point of explaining all this? It is much too difficult to explain in this atmosphere of electoral passion. I merely said: "You know perfectly well that at this moment you are acting like a scoundrel." That's all I said. What more was there to say?

I feel that the barriers are hardening, that the hatred around me is becoming more dense. But I also know that I will not give up the sunlight. In coming here I walked into a trap.

I can no longer stand slander, insults, and this unbearable inactivity. I cannot live outside love. I love my country more than all these people put together. They only love themselves. How odd is this destiny slipping downward like a mountain, without my being able to do anything about it. I have nothing to reproach myself for, no gesture of hate or malice, no self-seeking measures; not ten lines written for gain.

* During the war Henri Laugier was president of France Forever in the United States.

† See above, January 1941.

Nevertheless, I feel slowly but surely smothered. It's very odd indeed.

A journey perhaps? But I'm already in the quicksand up to my knees. It would be nothing short of a miracle if I managed to extract my legs. By tomorrow I shall have sunk in up to my stomach. That leads straight to prison.

But that is where they show themselves weak, because if I prefer to sleep, who is to stop me?

I think I shall burn my book.* If my papers are stolen, I don't want them lying around in their dirty offices.

My grief is beyond expression. . . .

. . .

You see, I just cannot understand life. At night I worry about everything: those I love, my country, the things I love.

I can't forget the miraculous peace of my last night in Libya. Talk to me, make me love life. I seem happy when performing card tricks, but I can't amuse myself with card tricks, only others. I feel so cold at heart.

. . .

My vertebra is agony. Pélissier is a bit sheepish about the fracture. It's not a fracture necessitating complete rest, it seems. It is a transverse fracture of the fifth lumbar vertebra. But I believe there is something else. And Pélissier, who advocates "ultra-penetrating" rays, doesn't interest me. He says, "That will cure your pain," but I don't care about the pain. I care about the signs.

There is a friendly element in pain. Like a familiar companion it is very, very faithful.

What I fear is anguish—and those I can no longer join. I

* The early stages of *The Wisdom of the Sands*.

worry about them. The same recurring theme of wanting to "save." If I'm prevented from rejoining them, I will carry all their misery in my heart. What I'm afraid of is my sleepless nights.

. . .

I'm worried about my book. How can I let all this be sullied? If one looks for praiseworthy arguments, one can find anything one likes. General Laugier is the best proof of that, but it cuts me to the quick.

But sometimes at least I have a chance to feel clear-cut pain in my vertebra. It doesn't hurt enough to really console me.

Tonight I should like to cry my heart out. The only thing preventing me is the comic side of it. This farce, and Laugier on top of it all!

I have a certain social sense. I've never been wrong about this. For two years now I have "known" all. I don't care about myself, but I am five hundred thousand Frenchmen. And I know that I'm thinking straight.

. . .

Three days later. It's cold. My vertebra hurts. There's no heat at Pélissier's (there's no chimney). My teeth are chattering. I wear two pairs of pajamas, a pair of underpants, and a dressing gown. In this way, I manage to pass the night comfortably. It's during the daytime that the lack of heat becomes a nuisance.

. . .

Perhaps I should go to prison—without killing myself. I have to pay off some enormous unknown debt.

What bothers me about Laugier is dishonor. I don't like dishonor. Imprisoned as an ally of torturers—that would bother me. That doesn't accord with anything that I believe. Perhaps it is worthwhile being imprisoned for one's own religion—but a very odd thing to be imprisoned for someone else's.

. . .

Prison—why not? I must be mad to want to kill myself. (But that's my anguish, which I cannot get the better of.) The question is: How much can I stand? Perhaps much more than I think. (But I already put up with so much!)

Perhaps this is sanctifying.

Long live God, as you said.

. . .

If I have vaguely learned how to write, it is because I am painfully aware of my errors. No phrase is ever safe. My old saying is not foolish: I don't know how to write; I only know how to correct.

. . .

Gaullism in a nutshell?

A group of "individuals" fight outside defeated France, which has to save its very essence. That's all well and good. France must take part in the fight.

And the general of this foreign legion would have had me as a soldier. But that group of "individuals" imagines that it represents France. France is represented by Tréfouël or Didi.*

They hope to benefit from a smaller sacrifice than their own, but there is true sacrifice only when no benefit accrues.

Because this group is taking part in the fight outside France and constitutes a normal "foreign legion," it claims the reward of ruling the France of tomorrow. It's absurd. The essential characteristic of sacrifice is that it claims no rights. That is the main point.

* His sister Gabrielle d'Agay.

It is absurd, because the France of tomorrow must arise—
if it arises at all—out of its own substance, which has provided
the prisoners, the hostages, the children dead of hunger. That
too is essential.

Their Assembly? They act very well, only the play they act
in is ridiculous. They believe they are France, when they should
be merely French, which is something quite different!

. . .

Cot, on returning from the United States, to the Great Mogul: "You are wrong. The United States is important. Roosevelt
is more French than all the Republicans put together. In the
interests of France, Roosevelt must be supported, not denigrated.
We must initiate a policy of friendship toward the United States."

"After all the U.S. has done to me!"

So tiresome—individuals who walk around with their ped-
estal under their arm, so tiresome to those who must watch.

. . .

Have you written to me? If so, what did you say? I've
received nothing in reply to my letter. Beware of entrusting a
letter to anyone, even messengers. People are lazy and they mail
the letter once they get here, as there is a lack of cars. And that's
like publishing a poster.

. . .

"He's nice, very nice, but he must be shot."

"Why?"

"It's because of him that General de Gaulle has not been
recognized by the United States."

Really? How flattering! How pleased I am with myself!

Oh, my Lord, human beings . . .

. . .

That fat idiot S.

"They wanted to shoot you in Brazil."

"Really?"

He always was an idiot, but he's only recently become fat. "Disgrace is fattening"—it sounds like a slogan.

He forgets to mention that it's because of him, the fat imbecile. One of the things that annoyed me in America was that he misquoted *Flight to Arras* in his speeches! He imputed arguments to it in order to serve his stupid, weak policies. This worm S. is not much nobler than Henri-Haye.* Whatever you express, the bastards join up with you and hold you up as a rallying sign. All the rebels and bankrupts of South America were Gaullists. It added to their stature. The collaborationist worms tried to appropriate *Flight to Arras* (by falsifying the text). That's what men are like!

. . .

A group commander said in the mess in front of the Great Mogul's portrait: "Replace the missing tacks! And add glass and a frame, so that at least it looks decorative."

"At least" . . . For that he got two weeks in the guardhouse!

A colonel remarked in a mess in Dakar, "There were more wounded in the Tunisian army than there were soldiers in de Gaulle's army." (Which is true.)

The colonel was downgraded. They have reinvented the crime of lèse majesté and the law on sacrilege. It's Nazism pure and simple.

. . .

How do you want me to carry on under such circumstances?

. . .

* Gaston Henri-Haye, Vichy's ambassador to the United States.

"Grief takes my breath away."

I said that softly to myself, as if it were poetry. I want to complain a little. What I wrote about Libya is true. On the morning of the last day, when the parachutes were dry* and I thought that I was going to die, I consoled myself for ten minutes, without moving, by repeating a sentence that seemed radiant to me: "Here is a dried-out heart, a dried-out heart that cannot produce tears!"

And now I tried to console myself for the present by repeating softly to myself, as I lay curled up in bed, trying to get to sleep: "Grief takes my breath away."

But such phrases are like Chinese fish. Once out of the water, they no longer resemble anything. And so it is outside of dreams . . .

Nevertheless it's true. Grief takes my breath away. . . .

. . .

12-24-43
Christmas Eve

At my uncle Emmanuel's at La Mole, there was an extraordinary Christmas crib with sheep, horses, an ox, shepherds, a donkey, and three Magi ten times larger than the horses, and above all a smell of heated wax that to me is the essence of any feast. I was five years old.

The gratitude of the world for the birth of a little child is something extraordinary—two thousand years later! The human species gathered together, knowing it must bring forth its miracle as a tree bears fruit. That is poetry.

The Magi, are they legend or history? In any case, it's a pretty tale.

. . .

---

* Saint-Exupéry, almost dying of thirst after his forced landing, spread out his parachutes on the sand in order to try and catch the dew.

Curiously, I thought of prison. I was stretched out and musing, trying to think of a card trick that would enable me to make good my escape. One does this and that and the trick is done.

But should this ill luck befall me, I will certainly not escape. I don't think I'll feel any urge to do so. One bears it to the bitter end. The escaped convict is outside his destiny and exists nowhere. He's ceased to count.

. . .

Corniglion-Molinier has suggested that I go to Russia with him in January or February. I've accepted. After all, I have to be somewhere, and there at least my age won't count so far as the war is concerned. What will have happened by then in this Algerian cesspool?

. . .

My back is becoming more and more painful. I'm still refusing Pélissier's "ultra-penetrating" radiation. The idea of radiation as treatment for a fracture irritates me.

Obviously I'm no longer any good for the infantry, but then I never did enjoy walking very much. I was always very heavy on my feet. At twenty-five I had those four years of rheumatism—then Guatemala and all the rest.

Perhaps the airplane was a strange compensation for me. . . .

. . .

Of course I should work, but where? And how? And why, if I am to burn all my efforts?

Maybe nothing will happen, but that doesn't mean that I'm wrong. Since you've been living there, you must have noticed something of this hatred that you only smiled at when I first mentioned it. They are merely weighing up whether or not it will be held against them in America—that's all. But as for that . . .

When such hatred comes from someone like Laugier it's quite natural. He hates me no more than I despise him. I abominate everything about his way of thinking, his scheming attitude toward people, his false expertise which understands nothing but claims to resolve everything, his tranquil acquiescence in baseness and stupidity. And he's supposed to have been a child at one time? Quite impossible. He was born with a monocle.

But when this hatred against me comes from a high-minded and upright individual it demoralizes me. Like a misunderstanding between lovers. I can't bear the powerlessness of words. I lose all faith in anything I can't express.

I've always thought that words were like love among tortoises—something not well attuned as yet. It may be in thirty million years' time. They will have acquired gracefulness. Just as we shall understand each other by mere hints.

They must have two different camps in order to make things out.

S. is on my side, since I'm not a Gaullist. It's a pity, because I'm not on his. Earlier, I didn't really know this spineless bishop, this lukewarm snail. I hate lukewarmness. His attitude in Brazil was poor. A sickly mess that swallowed everything. He "made me his own"—what a pity! But you can't prevent that. One is always infested with vermin.

. . .

My worries about others hit me each time like the stab of a knife. Suddenly, someone dear to me is present, surrounded by her particular danger "with nothing but four little thorns to defend herself with." Then someone else appears. But I can't possibly swim in several directions at once. Or rather, I can't swim at all. But prison, no doubt, is like a monastery. I might perhaps be at peace if I were the most unhappy one of all. That is why, strangely enough, my vertebra reassures me a little. And I know that if I were in great pain, I should be completely at peace.

And I know that if I were to die I should have an impression of being cared for; that stems from childhood. You are kissed and tucked into bed in order to get you to sleep.

But there's something else. Suddenly, any she and any he are "one and the same thing"—alike to all men, like virtue and vice, like birth and death as seen from the monastery of Solesmes. In a way, dying is like marrying. During my last night in Libya all that I loved was "accessible."

It's very strange.

. . .

It seems that I'm being looked for so that one of your letters can be given to me. I'm trying to find the messenger.

I've thought of several things. It's very curious—seen from Sirius—that one's inner climate should be transformed by a letter. This happens in music: One is steeped in Bach and one's behavior changes. If one were to die, then one's death would take on another dimension—or one's action—or one's misery.

The extraordinary value of "witness"—it's very strange. In fact, I am acknowledged by Johann Sebastian Bach when he speaks to me. The other day I received a letter that touched me. I was "acknowledged" by my correspondent. And that letter would have been more powerful than any prison wall. Its radiance would have melted any prison. The letter was not written by someone for whom I would readily die; nevertheless this person took on a sort of universal importance.

And God is threatened thereby—and threatened by another correspondent who writes to me about Bach: God, who simply "is." Bach would have achieved what this letter has achieved.

It's not really very different. And of course it seems to me that I can no longer live without her. But if another were to write to me, I should be equally unable to live without her. I say to myself immediately, "There is my thirst," because there is where it is quenched. But if it were Bach or an old fifteenth-century song, I would also say "There is my thirst." In the end my thirst reaches out—through all of them and all Bachs—toward an essential common denominator that I cannot perceive.

. . .

The arrival of all the books from America, except my own. BANNED IN NORTH AFRICA.

. . .

I'm a good example because I suffer cruelly. Misunderstandings and worry hurt me instantly like the stab of a knife. Certain words soothe me instantly.

I think it is a question of individuals. I have the illusion of love (I'm also capable of the illusion of hatred, and I always hate those who don't understand or who spread gossip, like L.), but the illusion is to assign that love or that hatred to the individual. The longer I live, the clearer it becomes to me that what is illusory is not love, but its object. There are only paths—and similarity between those who follow them. In the case of the individual I'm quickly bored. Each is a church to pray in, but not all day. God comes and goes.

The individual—like an hour of prayer. (But how few of them!)

. . .

I'm amazingly alone except for these few flashes.

. . .

The only thing in the world that really interests me becomes evident to me only in flashes and I cannot seize it. The burn caused by music, a picture, or love. That's why I think so much about Christmas, which embodies the year's meaning. And I know that year is bound to seem empty. It has no significance beyond this feast. And I can judge nothing by its materials.

That's why I'm irked when they analyze the stones along the path, or such and such a gesture. Because I find all the words and gestures ugly.

They reproach me for not condemning "this"—of course I condemn it, but also its opposite and them with it, and Darlan and Laugier too. Moreover, I refuse to exalt one in order to serve another. They are birds of a feather, base both of them.

A certain destiny makes itself felt through them whoever they are, and without their knowing it. Am I to blame if every movement of mankind turns ignoble at the tax and police level— if all gods are plagued by vermin—if the cathedral is built with the same stones as the brothel? I don't give a damn what reasons someone like Laugier has to hate the others—as much reason as Peyrouton has for hating Laugier. How much do they see of what may be developing beyond their miserable squabbles? I don't give a damn about their disputes. My only passion is for the invisible goal. That doesn't mean that I know the trick of how to bring it about. It merely means that their level revolts me.

. . .

J. came here and impressed me, although I cannot stand that kind of gangster, or his wife. All those drug-pushing heroes, gangsters, black marketeers. But successful libel, simplification, and slander are always very impressive.

How in the world could I even wish to explain to him how much more deeply I hated the Vichy regime than he did? . . .

I understand why all those who were animated by the spirit kept silent during their trial before being burned, decapitated, or crucified. The spirit arouses a passion that is unable to speak.

Even if I am able to see the future cathedral by looking at the pile of building stones, how can I show it to others before it has been constructed?

In fact, I don't even want to kill. I just shrug my shoulders and grieve.

1944

Letter to his Mother[1]

[January 5, 1944*]

Dearest Mama, Didi, and Pierre,† all of you whom I love so much—how are you, how are you getting along, what are you thinking? This long winter is so unutterably sad.

Nevertheless, in a few months' time I hope with all my heart to be folded in your arms, my darling little old Mama, to sit with you by the fire, telling you all I think, trying to contradict you as little as possible, listening to you—you who have been right about everything in life. . . .

I love you, dearest Mama.

Antoine

---

* This letter reached Mme de Saint-Exupéry via M. Dungler, one of the leaders of the Alsatian Resistance, who was parachuted into Clermont-Ferrand in January 1944.

† Pierre d'Agay, husband of Saint-Exupéry's sister Gabrielle (Didi).

Letter to X[2]

[Algiers, January 10, 1944]

Saw the messenger again. Strange. I'd like to get to know her writing. "I, I, I" is tiresome. The most odious "I" is "I said." She spoke her mind freely to the president, the king, the gendarme, the colonel, the fireman, the streetsweeper.

Courage. Such high-strung individuals are generally courageous—out of defiance. She defies the king, the president, the gendarme, the colonel, the fireman, the streetsweeper. She finds Algiers intolerable: She's doubtless right. She also finds the Americans, the Japanese, the inhabitants of Monaco or the Berry, the Negroes, the Indians, the Hindus, the Russians, the Germans, the Martians, the Kanakas, impossible. God, what a nuisance she can be.

She has no doubt rendered great services to the Resistance. This kind of individual would boldly carry around a shortwave radio under the very nose of the Gestapo. A person like her has masculine courage. What she does may be worthwhile, but nothing she says is of any interest. She told me at length how bitterly insulted she was when the information she passed on was not believed. She kept England informed about the bombing of viaducts, but it was not her they listened to. They only believed those who exaggerated in order to curry favor, speaking of massive destruction where none had occurred. She had proof of it, ample proof. . . . But there's such a thing as aerial photography. There is never a bombardment without aerial photographs afterward—one can almost count the missing bolts of a bridge. These photographs are extraordinarily precise and give more detailed information than an inspection on the spot—and they are quicker. Neither she nor her rivals were listened to; the intelligence services calmly made stereoscopic photomontages of aerial photographs.

A decent sort at heart, no doubt—but exhausting. Zero.

This evening I'm in a rage, which will turn into sadness tomorrow. I am enraged because all my work during the last month has come to nothing. General d'Astier de la Vigerie spoke for me. Bouscat* (who is no hero) had agreed once more to suggest my departure for England, but from a different angle. Things dragged on mysteriously. All was in fact so simple, useful, and clear.

But this evening Colonel Escarra, in charge of relations with foreign missions, phoned me.

"Is something wrong?"

"The Chief . . ."

"I see. He vetoed it?"

A blank wall. . . .

My crime is always the same: I proved in America that one could be a patriotic Frenchman, anti-German, anti-Nazi, and yet not approve of a future French government headed by de Gaulle and his party. And this is no small matter. France should decide. Abroad one can serve France, but not rule her. Gaullism should be a fighting weapon serving France—but it would be insulting the Gaullists to tell them so. During the last three years, I've never heard them talk of anything but governing France. But I'm not prepared to betray my integrity. France is neither Vichy nor Algiers. France is in the cellars. Let her choose the men of Algiers if she so wishes—but they have no special right.

* General René Bouscat was given command of the French Air Force in 1943. He had thought of assigning Saint-Exupéry to the Air Force Section of the French Military Mission in the United States. This assignment was considered "inopportune" by General de Gaulle (mid-December). Then General d'Astier de la Vigerie thought of using Saint-Exupéry in England, but in the end he did not consider it "opportune" and did not propose it to de Gaulle (early January 1944).[3]

I'm sure she will vote them in through hatred for the Vichy regime, and through ignorance of what they basically represent. That is the misfortune of an age that lives in darkness. We won't avoid a Terror, and that Terror will act in the name of an unformulated creed—the worst situation of all.

But (according to them) I refused to put the "enormous" prestige I had in America at their service. So I was the one responsible for their failure in the United States. It's because of me that they are not yet heading a government. It's truly comical! What a beautiful construction, built by political passion! How flattering!

And how it justifies the bulky dossiers that are piling up over my head. What a splendid discovery they made. It makes me sick. . . .

Saint-Exupéry was forced to endure inaction while the Americans landed at Anzio (January 22) and, together with the British, began the attacks on Cassino, which were to last until May. He worked on The Wisdom of the Sands.

Note to Georges Pélissier[4]

Algiers [1944]

I swear that I'm not being a damned nuisance. For three weeks now, I've been working on the idea for a film of *The Little Prince*. The intermediary, who is now on his way to London, came to pick up the book before leaving. The copy was nowhere to be found. And yet I haven't lent it to anyone, knowing that I would need it today.

That you should be unwilling to tell me what happened, that you shouldn't have a minute to devote to something that is vital to me and worth $50,000, is incomprehensible to me. God knows, I'm not being unfriendly. But if I stand to lose

\$50,000 in five minutes, it is surely worth thirty seconds of conversation.

Where is my book?

Letter to Georges Pélissier[5]

[1944]

Dear old friend,

Please don't think I bear you a grudge. If you had lent my book to someone else (when I never lend the only copy of something to anyone, but make them read it in my room), I would bear you a grudge. But that you should have borrowed it for yourself, I find very touching.

It so happens that this put me in a very awkward position. You may or may not know what the film industry is like. Business deals are either concluded on the spot immediately, or not at all—they cannot wait. I had just put together a scheme that depended on the book being read in London tomorrow. I was having lunch with the intermediary, who was leaving for London this afternoon. Of course, I forgot to bring the book with me and came back to pick it up before his plane left for Tangier.

Three films, after a hundred efforts, show that no success is ever assured and the chances of my selling my book—despite promising appearances—were 1 in 33. Nevertheless it was worth trying. The collapse of my whole scheme explains my letter. But it would never have been written had you not refused to waste thirty seconds of conversation to explain the matter, which, rightly or wrongly, I considered essential.

Your letter has reassured me about our friendship—the rest is unimportant. You were right to write to me. I prefer that the man should have left without the book rather than that you should not have written to me.

Forget my explosion—as would only be fair.

Note to Georges Pélissier[6]

[Ten minutes later]

I didn't properly explain what I found reassuring about your letter.

There can be no contest between friendship and anything else. I couldn't buy a friend for a hundred million. If you feel like rereading my book, I couldn't care less if Mr. Korda* had to wait and gave up on me. You have an absolute priority. There's no generosity in this. I couldn't buy your friendship for ten of Mr. Korda's films. Mr. Korda's money is worth what it can buy: not much. Nothing.

But I couldn't accept the thought of losing the advantages Mr. Korda has to offer just so some young nitwit I don't care a damn about should read my book. That was the reason for my automatic despair, which I should never have felt had I known that you wished to reread my little book.

You had a perfect right to do so.

But how could I have known?

Letter to Georges Pélissier[7]

[1944]

Dear old friend,

I sleep late because I've never been able to work except at night and I need seven hours' sleep on the average. But I don't mind getting up at 4, 5, 6, 7, 8, or 9 o'clock—especially since, if nothing urgent has come up on the telephone, I immediately go to sleep again.

In this stupid life that Le Troquer† makes me lead, I ob-

---

* Alexander Korda, Hungarian-born film producer active in Britain in the 1930s–1950s.

† André Le Troquer, Commissioner for War and the Air Force, whom Saint-Exupéry here uses as a symbol of the government that kept him grounded.

viously prefer to write at night (I can't write during the day because of the bustle and interruptions) and sleep in the morning. But I'm always at the disposal of anyone who needs me and I feel very awkward when it's said that I don't want to be disturbed in the morning.

That happened this morning because, in your friendly way, you wished to let me sleep. But I beg you in future not to take any account of the fact that I'm asleep. (It's the same in your case at the hospital.) If you are not up yet, I can go into your study or the drawing room without disturbing you in the least. You see, I'd rather not sleep for six nights than have anyone think (especially where my profession is concerned) that I'm reluctant to be disturbed before 10 A.M. That makes me seem like a pretty woman and quite ridiculous. Always wake me without the slightest scruple, even if I've only just gone to bed. My work at night has nothing to do with my correspondents. Thanks.

Finally Saint-Exupéry was sent back to his squadron, thanks to his friends Chambe, Chassin, Bouscat, Grenier, Frenay, and perhaps others.

John Phillips, a war correspondent for Life, *had asked him to write an article. Saint-Exupéry agreed in exchange for help in getting back to his squadron. As soon as that was accomplished, he wrote "Letter to an American."*

Letter to an American

I left the United States in 1943 in order to rejoin my fellow flyers of *Flight to Arras*. I traveled on board an American convoy. This convoy of thirty ships was carrying fifty thousand of your soldiers from the United States to North Africa. When, on waking, I went up on deck, I found myself surrounded by this city on the move. The thirty ships carved their way powerfully through the water. But I felt something else besides a sense of power. This convoy conveyed to me the joy of a crusade.

Friends in America, I would like to do you complete justice. Perhaps, someday, more or less serious disputes will arise between us. Every nation is selfish and every nation considers its selfishness sacred. Perhaps your feeling of power may, someday, lead you to seize advantages for yourselves that we consider unjust to us. Perhaps, sometime in the future, more or less violent disputes may occur between us. If it is true that wars are won by believers, it is also true that peace treaties are sometimes signed by businessmen. If therefore, at some future date, I were to inwardly reproach those American businessmen, I could never forget the high-minded war aims of your country. I shall always bear witness in the same way to your fundamental qualities. American mothers did not give their sons for the pursuit of material aims. Nor did these boys accept the idea of risking their lives for such material aims. I know—and will later tell my countrymen—that it was a spiritual crusade that led you into the war.

I have two specific proofs of this among others.

Here is the first.

During this crossing in convoy, mingling as I did with your soldiers, I was inevitably a witness to the war propaganda they were fed. Any propaganda is by definition amoral, and in order to achieve its aim it makes use of any sentiment, whether noble, vulgar, or base. If the American soldiers had been sent to war merely in order to protect American interests, their propaganda would have insisted heavily on your oil wells, your rubber plantations, your threatened commercial markets. But such subjects were hardly mentioned. If war propaganda stressed other things, it was because your soldiers wanted to hear about other things. And what were they told to justify the sacrifice of their lives in their own eyes? They were told of the hostages hanged in Poland, the hostages shot in France. They were told of a new form of slavery that threatened to stifle part of humanity. Propaganda spoke to them not about themselves, but about others. They were made to feel solidarity with all humanity. The fifty thousand soldiers of this convoy were going to war, not for the citizens of the United States, but for man, for human respect, for man's freedom and greatness. The nobility of your countrymen dictated the same nobility where propaganda was concerned. If someday your peace-treaty technicians should, for material and political reasons, injure something of France, they would be betraying your true face. How could I forget the great cause for which the American people fought?

This faith in your country was strengthened in Tunis, where I flew war missions for one of your units in July 1943. One evening, a twenty-year-old American pilot invited me and my friends to dinner. He was tormented by a moral problem that seemed very important to him. But he was shy and couldn't make up his mind to confide his secret torment to us. We had to ply him with drink before he finally explained, blushing:

"This morning I completed my twenty-fifth war mission. It was over Trieste. For an instant I was engaged with several Messerschmitt 109s. I'll do it again tomorrow and I may be shot down. You know why you are fighting: You have to save your country. But I have nothing to do with your problems in Europe. Our interests lie in the Pacific. And so if I accept the risk of being buried here, it is, I believe, in order to help you get back your country. Every man has a right to be free in his own country. But if I and my compatriots help you to regain your country, will you help us in turn in the Pacific?"

We felt like hugging our young comrade! In the hour of danger, he needed reassurance for his faith in the solidarity of all humanity. I know that war is indivisible, and that a mission over Trieste indirectly serves American interests in the Pacific, but our young comrade was unaware of these complications. And the next day he would accept the risks of war in order to restore our country to us. How could I forget such a testimony? How could I not be touched, even now, by the memory of this?

Friends in America, you see it seems that something new is emerging on our planet. It is true that technical progress in modern times has linked men together like a complex nervous system. The means of travel are numerous and communication is instantaneous—we are joined together materially like the cells of a single body, but this body has as yet no soul. This organism is not yet aware of its unity as a whole. The hand does not yet know that it is one with the eye. And yet it is this awareness of future unity which vaguely tormented this twenty-year-old pilot and which was already at work in him.

For the first time in the history of the world, your young men are dying in a war that—despite all its horrors—is for them an experience of love. Do not betray them. Let them dictate their peace when the time comes! Let that peace resemble them! This war is honorable; may their spiritual faith make peace as honorable.

I am happy among my French and American comrades. After my first missions in P-38 Lightnings they discovered my age. Forty-three years! What a scandal! Your American rules are inhuman. At forty-three years of age one doesn't fly a fast plane like the Lightning. The long white beards might get entangled with the controls and cause accidents. I was therefore unemployed for a few months.

But how can one think about France unless one takes some of the risks? There they are suffering, fighting for survival—dying. How can one judge those—even the worst among them—who suffer bodily there, while one is oneself sitting comfortably in some propaganda office here? And how can one love the best among them? To love is to participate, to share. In the end, by virtue of a miraculous and generous decision by General Eaker, my white beard fell off and I was allowed back into my Lightning.

I rejoined Gavoille, of *Flight to Arras*, who is in charge of our squadron in your Reconnaissance Group. I also met up again with Hochedé, also of *Flight to Arras*, whom I had earlier called a saint of war and who was then killed in war, in a Lightning. I rejoined all those of whom I had said that under the jackboot of the invader they were not defeated, but were merely seed buried in the silent earth. After the long winter of the armistice, the seed sprouted. My squadron once again blossomed in the daylight like a tree. I once again experience the joy of those high-altitude missions that are like deep-sea diving. One plunges into forbidden territory equipped with barbaric instruments, surrounded by a multitude of dials. Above one's own country, one breathes oxygen produced in America. New York air in a French sky—isn't that amazing? One flies in that light monster of a Lightning, in which one has the impression not of moving in space but of being present simultaneously everywhere on a whole continent. One brings back photographs that are analyzed by stereoscope like growing organisms under a microscope. Those analyzing your photographic material do the work of a bacteriologist. They seek on the surface of the body (France) the traces of the virus that is destroying it. The enemy forts, depots, convoys show up under the lens like minuscule bacilli. One can die of them.

And the poignant meditation while flying over France, so near and yet so far away! One is separated from her by centuries. All tenderness, all memories, all reasons for living are spread out 35,000 feet below, illuminated by sunlight, and nevertheless more inaccessible than any Egyptian treasures locked away in the glass cases of a museum.

Antoine de Saint-Exupéry

Letter to Mme François de Rose[8]

[May 1944]

Dear Yvonne,

I have to thank you for many things—I don't know what they are (the things that count are invisible), but I'm right no doubt, since I feel like thanking you.

That's not exactly it—one doesn't thank a garden. I've always divided human beings into two categories: those who resemble a courtyard and suffocate you between their walls—whom you are forced to speak to in order to make a noise because silence is painful in a courtyard.

Then there are those who resemble a garden, where you can walk, and be silent, and breathe. One feels at ease and experiences pleasant surprises. There is nothing to look for: a butterfly, a scarab, a glowworm appear. One knows nothing of the life habits of the glowworm. One muses. The scarab seems to know where it's going. It's in a great hurry. That is surprising. Then when the butterfly settles on a large flower, one says to oneself: "It's as if it landed on the terrace of one of the hanging gardens of Babylon, swaying gently to and fro." Then one is silent because of three or four stars.

In fact, I don't thank you at all—you are yourself and I feel like taking a stroll with you.

There are also people who resemble main roads and people who resemble country paths. The former bore me with their tarmac and their milestones. They lead somewhere definite— toward a profit or an ambition. Along the country paths there are nut trees instead of milestones, and one strolls along in order to crunch nuts—for no other reason. There is no set purpose, no ulterior motive. One walks along in order to take a stroll. But nothing is to be got out of milestones.

Yvonne, dear Yvonne, people in this day and age are on the wrong track. The telephone civilization is intolerable. True presence is replaced by a travesty of presence. One switches from one to the other in a second, as one switches the radio, by pressing a button, from Bach to a vulgar ditty. One is enfolded in nothing, one is nowhere. I hate this dissolvable humanity. Where I am, I am for all eternity. If I sit down on a bench, I want to remain there for all eternity. Sitting on my bench I am entitled to five minutes of eternity.

Of course you meet too many people. It's irritating and they pump you dry. And no doubt at night you are deeply discouraged—or would be if the telephone didn't prevent you from thinking by keeping you busy. And yet, curiously, one finds time with you. If it's only for a second, you have a second available. You are "there," present in your handshake, in your "How do you do?" or your good-bye, even. You are only pressed for time in between events. But within yourself you keep to the slow rhythm of a garden. I find this true rhythm so precious.

That is, no doubt, because you are undissolvable. But take care. It is very wearing to push radio buttons constantly, even if one is more or less undissolvable—even if one knows how to confine oneself in a second of Bach's music for all eternity. Idiots are very dangerous—so are intelligent people, if they are in a group. A single intelligence is a route, a hundred intelligences constitute a public square—a desperate thing without meaning.

I'm like an old man with a white beard, nodding his head— as if he regretted his youth spent sitting on top of bullock carts. I must have once been a Merovingian king, though I've been on the move all my life, and I'm tired of running. It's only now that I can understand a certain Chinese proverb: "Three things destroy the ascent of the spirit. First of all, travel . . ." And Derain* told me twenty times, "I've only known three truly great men. They were all illiterate: a Savoyard shepherd, a fisherman, a beggar. They had never left their surroundings,

---

* André Derain (1880–1954), French painter of the Fauve school.

but they are the only men I met in all my life that I admired."

Poor José Laval, on her return from the United States, made this charming remark: "I'm glad to be back. I'm not on the same scale as skyscrapers, but rather on the scale of a donkey."

And I'm sick of milestones that lead nowhere. It is high time to be reborn.

While waiting for the vocation to enter Solesmes (Gregorian chant is fine) or a Tibetan monastery, or to become a gardener, I am once again pulling throttles and speeding along to nowhere at four hundred miles per hour.

That is why, dear Yvonne, I've written this letter, which doesn't mean much and is probably illegible (I'm too old to improve my writing). But it doesn't matter. I just wanted to take a rest for five minutes of eternity in friendship.

Saint-Exupéry

Don't bother to answer me as I don't believe letters ever reach this godforsaken country. I will be coming to Algiers soon. I'll phone. A plane is leaving which is taking this letter.

On June 4 General Mark Clark and General Alphonse Juin were in Rome. On June 6 the Allied landing in Normandy took place. Saint-Exupéry heard of it on returning from a mission aborted due to engine trouble.

On June 14 he at last flew over France—the area around Rodez. It was his first flight over France since rejoining his squadron.

Letter to General Chambe or General Brosset[9]

Algiers [July 3, 1944]

Dear General,

Thank you for sending me the only copy I possess of *Flight to Arras*, which arrived safely. I don't know what your reflections were on reading it, or whether it modified the reactions of the commander (whose name I forget) who attacked me so suddenly but in a pleasant manner during our breakfast meeting. I was impressed not so much by his aggressiveness as by his integrity, and I wanted very much for him to reread *Flight to Arras*.

As you don't mention any reaction on his part, I take it that he didn't understand what I wished to express. It seems strange to me that the climate of controversy these days should be such as to warp the meaning of such a simple text for someone so honest. I don't care if the noncombatants in Algiers dissect and debate my secret intentions. Those they ascribe to me are as much like me as I am like Greta Garbo. I'm completely indifferent to their opinion of me, even if it leads to the banning of my book in North Africa. I'm not a bookseller. On the other hand, your friend's misinterpretation is, oddly enough, unbearable—no doubt because I esteem him. It is for him and men like him that I wrote, not for politicians. Why did he read my few pages in the false light of a political creed? Imagine that I were Montaigne and published the *Essays* in an Algerian journal and that people insisted on explaining them in the light of the armistice problem—what Machiavellian maneuvers would they not discover in my book?

I spoke of responsibility, all right. But, good God, my meaning was clear! I didn't write a single line on the monstrous idea of the French being responsible for the defeat. I said clearly to the Americans: "You are responsible for the defeat. We were forty million people working on the land against eighty million working in industry. One man against two men, one machine tool against five. Even if a Daladier had reduced the French people to slavery, he could not have exacted a hundred daily working hours from each man. A day has only twenty-four hours. Whatever the management of France, the arms race would have resulted in one man pitted against two and one cannon against five. We were prepared to fight one against two—we were ready to die. But in order for our death to be effective, we needed you to give us the four tanks, the four cannon, the four planes that we lacked. You expected us to save you from the Nazi menace, but you went on producing Packards and refrigerators for your weekends. That is the sole cause of our defeat. But that defeat has nevertheless saved the world. The acceptance of our defeat was the starting point of the resistance against Nazism." I said to them (they were not yet at war): "The tree of resistance will one day grow out of our sacrifice as out of a seed!" Can your friend differ from me as regards this essential aspect of my book? The miracle was that the Americans read it and that it became a best seller. The miracle was that it led to a hundred newspaper articles in which the Americans themselves said, "Saint-Exupéry is right; we must not condemn France. We are partly responsible for her defeat." If Frenchmen in America had only followed my lead a little more instead of forever explaining everything by the rot of France, our relations with the United States would not be what they are today. No one will ever make me think any differently.

And yet there is a more general side to my book, where I do say, "We are responsible." But I'm not speaking of the defeat, rather of the fascist and Nazi phenomenon. I said (how on earth can this not be evident, I tried so hard to make myself understood!), I said: The Christian civilization of the West is responsible for the menace that hangs over it. What has it done in the last eighty years to bring its tenets alive in men's hearts? The only new ethic put forward was Guizot's "Prosper and amass riches" or the American idea of comfort. After 1918 what was there to exalt young men's hearts? My own generation played the stock exchange, discussed car models and their respective merits in bars, or made sordid business deals. How few experienced a monastic life of dedication such as I lived through with Aéropostale. How many sank into the dismal morass of card games and Pernod, or bridge and cocktail parties, according to their social group. For twenty years of my life, I've despised the plays of Bernstein* (that great patriot) and Louis Verneuil, but above all the selfish isolationism in the world, with everyone looking after his own interests. I wrote *Wind, Sand and Stars* in order to tell men passionately that they were all inhabitants of the same planet, passengers on the same ship. In what way are the fat prelates (who are collaborationists today) or the supreme magistrates trustees of Western Christian civilization, of its universal creed? Men felt a thirst that nothing on the Continent could satisfy. Don't you see that my deep friendship for you derived from the discovery at our first meeting that you were a man like me, a man after my own heart? You too were thirsty, and mysteriously our thirst could only be quenched in the desert, or at difficult moments during night flights. Neither of us could bear to read *Le Canard Enchaîné* or *Paris-Soir*. I couldn't stand Louis Verneuil. Why did your book appeal to me so profoundly? I need that manna. I love those who quench my thirst. I despise what Louis Philippe, Guizot, and Mr. Hoover have turned men into. It's a question of the perennial opposition between nomadic and sedentary peoples. Civilization must be saved continually. In Paraguay, which you know, the rain forest makes itself felt between every paving stone of the capital city, even if by no more than a blade of grass. But that blade of grass could swallow a town. The rain forest has to be driven back continually.

What was there for your friend (whom I think I understand) to find satisfying in the prewar ethic? And if, like us, he felt an unquenchable thirst, why in God's name does he feel indignation when I condemn those years for neglecting spiritual values? Why does he misinterpret and misconstrue my book? When I say that each of us is responsible for all, I am in the Augustinian tradition. So is your friend while he is fighting. He embodies

---

* Henri Bernstein (1896–1953), like Verneuil a fashionable French playwright who lived in the United States from 1940 to 1945.

the Breton peasant and the country postman at war. He is the arm that fights and through him the country postman is at war— through the country postman, your friend also serves the community. The whole cannot be divided into separate parts.

What possible connection can there be between the subject I've written about and the imbecile whining about Léon Blum's politics? Where is there in my book a single line that could justify equating my "I'm responsible" with a humiliating mea culpa? It should be the proud motto of everyone. It stands for belief in action. It is the basis of human feeling. That musty bureaucrats should read political intentions into my book makes me smile indulgently, because I was fighting every week over France alone in a P-38 Lightning despite my forty-four years, because I returned eight days ago pursued by fighter planes and had engine trouble over Annecy. I don't care about those bureaucrats. But I cannot accept that your upright friend should misinterpret my message. I wrote for him and those like him. Let him reread my book in ten years' time, since it seems impossible to get through to even the most upright minds today.

Letter to Georges Pélissier[10]

[Tunis,* July 9–10, 1944]

Dear friend,

I'm staying here for two days. My plane has mechanical trouble: "The electrical leads got crossed in the cables and the whole lot burned: starter, radio, etc." By the time this letter reaches you, I will no doubt be back in my dovecote.

Quite by chance, I heard that relations between Algiers and that dovecote were all but severed. Even if I should be away for longer, don't forward my letters—they would get lost. Never-

* During the month of July Saint-Exupéry went to Tunis six times.

theless, keep on trying to forward copies of any telegrams. Many thanks.

I leave tomorrow. I practice an odd profession for my age. The nearest one to me in age is six years younger. I much prefer this life in a tent or whitewashed room with breakfast at 7 A.M., the mess, and then flying at 35,000 feet in a different universe to the ghastly inactivity of Algiers. I cannot think or write in a provisional limbo. I lacked a social purpose there. But I've chosen the most wearing profession, and as one must always carry things through, I won't give up. I hope this sinister war will be over before I've melted away completely, like a candle burning in oxygen. I have other work to do later on.

Of course, I'm very attached to my fellow flyers in the squadron. And yet I suffer from lack of human contact. The mind and spirit are so important. In the mess, during meals, I have the bitter impression of a terrible waste of time. I can blend into any group. . . . And no one would guess that I lack anything whatsoever, except the movies and women, like the others. And yet the greatest part of myself is reduced to silence. And I lack everything. . . .

Letter to his Mother[11]

[Borgo, July 1944]

My dearest Mama,

I would like so much to reassure you about me and to be sure that my letter reaches you. I'm well, very well. But I'm sad not to have seen you for so long and I'm worried about you, my darling Mama. What an unhappy time we live in!

I was heartbroken to hear that Didi has lost her home. How I wish I could help her! But do tell her that she can count on me to help her in the future. When will it be possible to say to those one loves that one loves them?

My dearest Mama, love me as I love you.

Antoine

Letter to Pierre Dalloz[12]

[July 30 or 31, 1944]
Postal Sector 99027

Dear Dalloz,

. . . I fight as earnestly as I can. I must be the oldest fighter pilot in the world. The normal age limit for the type of fighter plane I fly is thirty. And the other day I had mechanical trouble while flying over Annecy at the precise moment I became forty-four years old! As I was crossing the Alps at a snail's pace pursued by German fighter planes, I smiled to myself while thinking of those superpatriots who banned my books in North Africa. How very odd life is.

I've experienced everything since my return to the squadron: engine trouble, fainting due to lack of oxygen, pursuit by enemy fighter planes, and fire on board during flight. I don't feel too avaricious, and I consider myself a sound craftsman. That is my only satisfaction—as well as being alone on board a solitary plane flying over France taking photographs. That's also strange.

One is far removed here from the pervasive hatred, but in spite of the comradeship within the squadron, there is the feeling of human frailty. I have no one, no one to talk to. At least there is someone to share life with. But what a spiritual desert!

If I'm shot down, I won't regret anything. The future anthill appalls me and I hate the robot virtues. I prefer to be a gardener.

Saint-Ex

On July 31 at 8:45 A.M., Saint-Exupéry took off to fly over Annecy.

INTERROGATION REPORT

MEDITERRANEAN ALLIED PHOTO RECONNAISSANCE COMMAND

Sortie No.	Date
XX 335 176	31 JULY 1944
Pilot	
Observer	Time out: 0845 Time in:
MAJ. ST EXUPERY	
Squadron	Total Time: E/A:
33RD FAF	
Aircraft No.	Flak:
223	
Targets and Reference . . .	Remarks . . .
M/F/A/428	
MAPPING EAST OF LYON	NO PICTURES

General Remarks

PILOT DID NOT RETURN AND IS PRESUMED LOST

[Vernon F. Robison, Liaison Officer]

In the squadron's day book, among other flights, there is the following entry:

Date: 31 July—*Crew:* Pilot. *Rank, name:*
Type and no. of plane: Lockheed P-38 no. 223.
Nature of aerial service: Photographic mission over Southern France.

Never returned. . . .

[*signature*] Gavoille René

Recollections of General René Gavoille[13]

. . . I won't see Saint-Exupéry again. On the afternoon of July 30, he was in Bastia, where he met Colonel Rockwell and some friends. He was sorry not to be able to stay on with them and invited them to our mess for the following evening, as he was already invited to dine that same evening at a restaurant a few kilometers from Erbalunga—a very gay dinner party, as some of the guests recall.

On July 31, Saint-Exupéry was on hand very early, contrary to his usual habit. Was it not the same on the night preceding his Paris–Saigon competition flight? He drove to the airstrip with Lieutenant Duriez, attached to Operations, and for the eleventh time during this 1943–4 period prepared for a mission: 33 S 176, mapping east of Lyons. . . . He took off at 8:45 A.M. in P-38 no. 223; I was told this on my arrival at the airstrip later in the morning. Everyone remembers my reaction. At 1 P.M. he had not returned. At 2:30 P.M., after numerous phone calls, radar and radio searches, there was no more hope of his still being airborne, and at 3:30 P.M. our American officer Robison signed the *Interrogation Report*, noting: *Pilot did not return and is presumed lost.*

It was the first time I had not been present while he was getting ready for a mission, dressing, then starting the engines, checking everything in the cockpit, having the blocks removed, seeing him off—for the mission that was to be his last.

In his room, where I went through his things with Captain Leleu, his bed was untouched; he had not been to bed and on the table lay two letters addressed to friends, including one to Pierre Dalloz (both had been written the day before).

Colonel Rockwell, a great friend of France, formerly of the Lafayette Escadrille, and others: Colonel Baralès, Major Marin, Captain Lachelier arrived at our mess in response to Saint-Exupéry's invitation of the previous evening and heard the sad news. . . .

Whole books have been written about Saint-Exupéry's disappearance. We know what happened or didn't happen on July 31. Our American and French records are precise. Radar indicated that Saint-Exupéry's plane did not cross the coast of Southern France on his return flight and that there was no combat over the sea. At first we hoped to see him return soon. But that hope faded progressively, despite our searches.

Recollections of Vernon F. Robison[14]

Gavoille stayed at my side all the time, still hoping. From time to time, he suggested some explanation or other for his late return. Perhaps he had made a forced landing or bailed out. Perhaps he had suffered from lack of oxygen and been forced to descend to an altitude below that of radar detection. Saint-Exupéry did in fact use up more oxygen than the other pilots. I know he always put the maximum effort into every mission. If he found his first objective covered in cloud, he went off to look for another, then returned or remained nearby until the sky cleared. This passion for perfection often made him return later than scheduled.

All these explanations that gave us reason for hoping against hope became less and less plausible as time went on. Only when it became evident that the plane's fuel capacity had long since run out did Gavoille with a very heavy heart tell us not to wait any longer.

There has always been speculation as to where and how Saint-Exupéry died. Various apparently relevant accounts have been gathered together. More and more of these have appeared as the years have gone by, not without contradicting each other.

One of the first to appear was that of the theology student Hermann Korth, an admirer of Saint-Exupéry's; it was published by Pierre Chevrier in 1949.[15]

At Malcesina on Lake Garda, Hermann Korth, a German officer of the *Luftflottenkommando 2*, was working in a hut among his telephone lines. For a month this young pilot, who had been shot down four times, had been confined to a desk. From 6 A.M. to midnight he kept a watch over a sector stretching from Belgrade to Avignon. On the morning of July 31, a Messerschmitt 109 and an F-W 190 were to take off from France to reconnoiter the airfield of Ajaccio.

At 5 P.M. Korth called "Tribun" (code word for Avignon), but it did not answer. The line was cut. At half past midnight, the officer put away his daily report. He was preparing to leave when the telephone rang. "Tribun," Avignon local headquarters, confirmed the return of the mission over Ajaccio of the Reconnaissance Group of Istres (*Nahaufklärungsgruppe 2*). The officer noted down the information in his personal notebook under date of July 31, 1944:

Anr[uf] Tribun K[ommandantur?] Abschuss 1 Aufkl[ärungsflugzeug] brennend über See. Aufkl[ärungsflug] Ajacc[io] unverändert.

Literally:

Telephone call from Tribun headquarters shot down one reconnaissance plane in flames over the sea.* Reconnaissance flight over Ajaccio unchanged.

---

* Was it Saint-Exupéry's plane? Jean Leleu says the following: "It seems that this plane must have been that of our American friend Meredith, who was shot down the previous day in the same type of plane, and whose crash was reported to Korth during the night of July 30–1. Korth relates that the message reached him when he had already gone to bed and that he only noted it down in his own notebook, which was lying on his bedside table, in order to copy it out the next day into the records. It is therefore probable that he transcribed it the next day, on July 31. Moreover, he reported only one plane shot down during those two days and Meredith's crash is certain (since the poor fellow radioed for help)." (*Icare*, no. 96, p. 139.) This is also the opinion of Curtis Cate, p. 530.

*The following account, by Junior Flying Officer (Oberfähnrich)
Robert Heichele, published in German in 1972, received a certain
amount of publicity in France and abroad in 1981.*[16]

On July 31, I took off (from the base at Orange) with Sergeant
Högel at 11:02 A.M. on a mission to observe enemy air activity
between Marseilles, Menton, and the hinterland. We carried out
our mission according to the orders given and as we made a
half-turn over Castellane, we encountered a P-38 Lightning. It
was probably an enemy reconnaissance plane flying alone. Since
the enemy was flying about 1,000 meters above us, we saw no
possibility of attacking him. To my utter surprise, the enemy
flew toward us and attacked us from above and at superior
speed.*

We avoided the first assault by a spiraling ascent and we
managed to gain an advantage over the P-38 by making use of
our extra auxiliary power.

During this aerial combat I was able to place myself in a
position to fire, behind the P-38. The distance was about 150–
200 meters. I fired, but the burst of gunfire passed to the rear
of the plane. I took another turn and once more placed myself
in a firing position. The distance was about 300 meters. The
burst of gunfire passed just in front of the plane. Probably in
order to avoid my fire, the pilot flew in a straight line and then
dropped down.

I pursued him and came nearer—the distance was about 40–
60 meters—I fired again. After that, I noticed that the Lightning
was losing altitude, leaving a white trail behind it. I followed
at a distance. The P-38 crossed the coast and flew out to sea

---

* This allegation can only be explained by a misunderstanding: Either the German
pilot, who was not a "qualified" fighter pilot, wanted to emphasize that he was forced
to join battle, or else the pilot of the P-38 voluntarily lost altitude in order to breathe
(the oxygen supply being sometimes unreliable) without becoming aware of the enemy
plane below him, which must have been camouflaged.

just above the waves. I followed the Lightning and suddenly flames shot out of the starboard engine. The right wing dipped, plowing into the sea. The plane somersaulted several times and sank. The crash occurred at 1205 hours, approximately 10 kilometers south of Saint-Raphaël, in map square AT. We returned without further contact with the enemy.

There is another account extant that rather poignantly corroborates the preceding one. It is by Claude-Alain Jaeger, who was a resident of Biot in 1944. The only element that differs in the two accounts is the place where the downed plane crashed into the sea. In any case, it is unlikely that German fighter planes would have shot down two P-38s at the same time and in the same area.

Recollections of Claude-Alain Jaeger[17]

In July 1944 I was a student of seventeen and a half, living in Biot in the Alpes Maritimes. I made a habit of noting down, day by day, various observations of a general military nature, from January 1, 1944, to August 24, 1944, the date of the liberation of France.

Here is what I wrote down on July 31: "Saw white trail at 3,000 meters at 11 A.M. At 12 noon low flight, sustained light anti-aircraft fire . . ." That was taken down in a Pestalozzi notebook (which was the standard pocket notebook of Swiss schoolchildren).

Description of the facts: Alerted by regular ground fire issuing from west of the village in the direction of the battery of Valmasque (probably a 20-mm anti-aircraft gun), I looked out of the window of my parents' apartment in Biot. The windows face toward Nice. Their field of vision is wide; one can see the summit of Courmette above Grasse on the left, and the sea (Biot station) to the right. The village of Biot is situated on a rock at an altitude of eighty meters. Facing these windows was a deep ravine about 400 meters wide.

I saw very distinctly coming from the direction of Grasse a completely silver plane with a double fuselage. The plane was flying at great speed toward the sea, 3,800 meters away. It was just above the height of the roofs. What struck me was that it had the American star painted on one wing and on its side the French tricolor insignia. No wing tanks. The pilot was wearing a dark flying suit. The sighting lasted several seconds (this was not yet the age of the jet). No smoke trail at the back of the plane, no engine trouble or puffs of anti-aircraft fire.

Commentary: Identification was easy, as I had seen pictures of the P-38 Lightning in *Science et Vie* and other journals, including the German weekly *Der Adler*. My mother, aged 76, also remembers the plane flying past, since she was looking out with me at the time. We thought: "What a fine American plane, but why the French insignia?"

Others at Biot saw this plane, but did not note down the day or time. These are M. Marcel Camatte, at present mayor of Biot, and Roger Léone.

Why did I not make this known earlier? First of all, I had mislaid my notebook, which I found again only in 1976. Also I did not make any connection [between Saint-Exupéry's disappearance and my observations]. I wrote to General Gavoille in 1977, because I had read one of his articles in a military journal. The general replied to me and, as research was able to establish, Saint-Exupéry's was the only P-38 on a mission that day in that zone.

General Gavoille has since received the account of another eyewitness, aged nine and a half at the time, who lived in the district of La Fontonne at Antibes, very near the Biot railway station.* One day at the end of July, it seems, that witness saw

---

* See article by General Gavoille, *Icare*, no. 96, p. 101.

a plane pursued by two others. The first plane was seen to be shot down opposite Cagnes-sur-Mer or Saint-Laurent-du-Var.

Commander Cousteau or the French Navy might be able to pinpoint the exact place where the plane dropped into the sea.

It was a beautiful day without a cloud. The sun was shining. It was too fine a day to die on. . . .

As has been explained earlier, the radar detectors reported nothing; therefore, the P-38 must have been flying very low.

A doubt remains as to the exact line of flight taken by the damaged plane and the exact point where it crashed into the sea, despite square AT on the map indicated by the German pilot.* It is possible that Saint-Exupéry flew over Biot and turned right, to the south of Saint-Raphaël, which would corroborate this detail in Heichele's account; or he may have continued his flight toward Monte Carlo, which would tally with the following account, by the German Major Leopold Böhm:†

It was the end of July 1944. I commanded the defense company in a zone extending from Villefranche to Monte Carlo. I was stationed in a villa at a place called Tête de Chien.‡ Since I was wounded, I had my bed put on the veranda in order to observe better, and there was never a dull moment. I had Hensold field glasses, which sometimes made it possible for me to see the waves breaking on the coast of Corsica. That day, I saw three dots appear on the horizon—three planes flying toward Monte Carlo. These three planes were cruising, skimming above the sea. They were heading straight for my command post. The

* Looking at the German map reproduced in *Icare*, no. 96, p. 157, one can see that square AT is southeast of Genoa. The squares south of Saint-Raphaël are CO and DO. Was this the division into squares used on that day, however?

† Quoted by Gavoille, *Icare*, no. 96, p. 101.

‡ Fortified position high above Monaco.

two pursuers forced the first one to crash-land on the waves, then they pulled out and disappeared.

The most credible accounts seem to be those of Claude-Alain Jaeger, Leopold Böhm, and Robert Heichele.

Notes

The following publications are cited in abbreviated form in the notes:

Antoine de Saint-Exupéry. *Lettres à sa mère*. Paris: Gallimard, 1955. References are to the revised edition (1965).
————. *Oeuvres*. Paris: Bibliothèque de la Pléiade, 1959.
————. *Un sens à la vie*. Text compiled and annotated by Claude Reynal. Paris: Gallimard, 1956. (*A Sense of Life*. New York: Funk & Wagnalls, 1965.)
Curtis Cate. *Antoine de Saint-Exupéry, laboureur du ciel*. Paris: Bernard Grasset, 1973. (*Antoine de Saint-Exupéry: His Life and Times*. New York: Putnam, 1970.)
Pierre Chevrier. *Antoine de Saint-Exupéry*. Paris: Gallimard, 1949.
————. *Saint-Exupéry*. Paris: Gallimard, "La bibliothèque idéale," 1958.
Pierre Dalloz. *Vérités sur le drame du Vercors*. Paris: Editions Lanore, 1978.

René Delange. *La Vie de Saint-Exupéry*. Paris: Editions du Seuil, 1958.

Georges Pélissier. *Les cinq visages de Saint-Exupéry*. Paris: Flammarion, 1951.

Léon Werth. *Déposition, Journal 1940–1944*. Paris: Grasset, 1946.

Confluences, vol. VII, no. 12–14 (1947).

Icare, revue de l'Aviation française. Saint-Exupéry series: no. 78, 1976 (vol. IV, 1939–40: la Seconde Guerre Mondiale, le Groupe de Reconnaissance II/33 jusqu'à l'Armistice); no. 84, 1978 (vol. V, 1941–3: Saint-Exupéry aux U.S.A., *Pilote de Guerre, Lettre à un otage, Le Petit Prince*); no. 96, 1981 (vol. VI, 1943–4: Retour au combat, Alger, la disparition de Saint-Exupéry).

1939

1. Rough draft, 1939; private collection.
2. "La paix ou la guerre" in *Paris-Soir,* October 2–4, 1938. Reprinted in *Un sens à la vie*, pp. 147–82. Quotation from the first article, "Homme de guerre, qui es-tu?," p. 147; and from the third article, "Il faut donner un sens à la vie des hommes," pp. 173–9.
3. Reprinted in *Un sens à la vie*, pp. 113–42.
4. Anne Morrow Lindbergh, *Le Vent se lève (Listen! The Wind)*, Paris: Correa (Buchet et Chastel), 1939; preface by Antoine de Saint-Exupéry, reprinted in *Un sens à la vie*, pp. 246–56.
5. Unpublished; printed by permission of the Institut National Audiovisuel.
6. Unpublished; private collection.
7. Unpublished; private collection.
8. Unpublished; private collection.
9. Unpublished; private collection.
10. See *Cahiers Saint-Exupéry*, I, 1980, pp. 47–60.

11. Unpublished; private collection.
12. Unpublished; private collection.

1940

1. Letter written from Orconte in 1940; quoted by Pierre Chevrier, 1949, p. 215.
2. Contributed to this volume.
3. Unpublished; private collection.
4. Unpublished; private collection.
5. Unpublished; private collection.
6. Unpublished; private collection.
7. Unpublished; courtesy of Dr. Claude Werth. See also Léon Werth, "Plus tard, la perfection de la mort," *Confluences*, p. 65; Léon Werth, "Saint-Ex tel que je l'ai connu," in René Delange, p. 185.
8. Jean Israël published this document in *Icare*, no. 78, pp. 62–3.
9. Facsimile in *Icare*, no. 78, p. 38.
10. Letter to Editions Gallimard.
11. Facsimile in *Icare*, no. 78, p. 53.
12. *Lettres à sa mère*, p. 166.
13. Ibid., p. 167.
14. Unpublished; private collection.
15. Facsimile in *Icare*, no. 78, p. 85.
16. *Lettres à sa mère*, p. 169.
17. Unpublished; private collection.
18. Curtis Cate, pp. 406–7.
19. Private collection; published by Chevrier, 1949, p. 230.

1941

1. Jean Renoir, "Il parlait toute la nuit," *Icare*, no. 84, p. 27.
2. Quoted by René Gavoille, "Il est des nôtres," *Icare*, no. 78, p. 28.
3. Unpublished; reproduced from a photocopy of the original,

by kind permission of Butler Library, Columbia University.

4. Unpublished; private collection.

5. Unpublished; Butler Library, Columbia University.

6. Unpublished; Butler Library, Columbia University.

7. This text was published by P. Aelberts, Liège, n.d.: reprinted in *Icare*, no. 84, pp. 118–9. It has been collated with the original, kindly lent by Butler Library, Columbia University. An English translation by Lewis Galantière was published on May 25, 1942, in *Senior Scholastic*, vol. 40, pp. 17–8.

8. The passage from "Hunchbacks" to "cult of humanity" appears in the original in the form of a handwritten note by Lewis Galantière.

9. This sentence is to be found in the manuscript but not in the printed text.

1942

1. The letters addressed to Mrs. Sylvia Reinhardt-Hamilton are analyzed and partially published in the Catalogue Drouot Rive Gauche of May 20, 1976. Facsimiles are to be found in *Icare*, no. 84, pp. 110ff. et seq.

2. Unpublished; Butler Library, Columbia University.

3. Unpublished; Butler Library, Columbia University.

4. Unpublished; private collection.

5. This version was published in *Un sens à la vie*, pp. 209–17; in Georges Pélissier, pp. 213–9; and in *Icare*, no. 84, pp. 122ff.

6. Published in Pélissier, p. 73.

1943

1. Contributed to this volume.

2. See Chevrier, 1958, pp. 70–1: ". . . Léon Werth had asked

Saint-Exupéry to write a preface for his book about the war. Saint-Exupéry, who did not wholeheartedly agree with the contents of the book, refrained from writing the preface. Unable at a distance to discuss in detail the points they differed on, he felt the need to express his friendship. This letter eventually developed into a book." *L'Amérique Française*, which printed part one of *Lettre à un otage* in March 1943, also described it as a preface ("Lettre à un ami"). The original typescript of part one is among the papers of Lewis Galantière, in Butler Library, Columbia University; Galantière translated it for *Collier's* magazine. On the library card it is described as a "preface" for Léon Werth's *Trente-trois jours*.

3. Léon Werth, *Déposition*.
4. Unpublished; private collection.
5. Contributed to this volume.
6. General René Chambe, *Icare*, no. 96, pp. 38–41.
7. Unpublished, n. d.; private collection. An extract was published in Chevrier, 1949, p. 261.
8. Catalogue Drouot Rive Gauche, May 20, 1976.
9. Chambe, "Retour au combat," *Icare*, no. 96, p. 39. The P-38 Lightning, a twin-fuselage fighter, was made by Lockheed. Saint-Exupéry flew the following versions of the plane: F-4 (from Laghouat), F-5A (from Alghero and Borgo), F-5B (last mission from Borgo). The P-38 had two engines of 1,150 horsepower each. Its top speed was about 400 mph, cruising speed about 300 mph. Maximum altitude was about 39,000 feet (on reconnaissance missions, 30,000 feet). Normal range was about 1,425 miles. The P-38 fighter carried an armament of four machine guns; these were removed from reconnaissance aircraft and cameras were installed in the nose of the plane. See E. Petit and François Rude, "Les avions de Saint-Exupéry," *Icare*, no. 96, 189–93; *Mach I,*

Encyclopédie de l'aviation, no. 80 (October 1, 1981), pp. 568–9.

10. Unpublished; from a photocopy of the original, in the possession of Harcourt Brace Jovanovich, Publishers.

11. Published in Pélissier, p. 40.

12. Ibid.

13. Published in *Le Figaro Littéraire*, April 10, 1948, later in pamphlet form as *Que faut-il dire aux hommes? Lettre au général X* (n.p., 1948). See also *Icare*, no. 96, pp. 31–41, 50–1. It is generally agreed that this letter was addressed to General Chambe. The letter was "the precise continuation of a conversation we had in Tunisia," Chambe explained in Richard Rumbold and Margaret Stewart, *Saint-Exupéry tel quel* (Paris: Del Duca, 1960), pp. 329–31.

14. Chambe, "Retour au combat," *Icare*, no. 96, p. 40.

15. See Pierre Massin de Miraval, "Le menu d'Alger," *Icare*, no. 96, p. 80.

16. Published in Pélissier, pp. 42–4.

17. Letter found in Saint-Exupéry's papers; excerpted several times, notably in *Le Monde*, July 29, 1950, and (more completely) in *Le Courrier de l'Ouest*, January 15, 1950. The latter journal received it from Catroux, who described the text as having been written by Saint-Exupéry "on the eve of his death." For details and a facsimile see Diomède Catroux, "Le laboureur et l'ingénieur," *Icare*, no. 96, pp. 70–3.

18. Published by Delange, pp. 234–5.

19. Unpublished; private collection.

20. Published in *Confluences*, p. 89; facsimile in *Icare*, no. 71, 1974–5, p. 92.

21. Henri Comte, "Histoire d'une lettre," with facsimile, *Icare*, no. 96, pp. 59–61. We wish to thank *Icare* for providing us with a copy of this letter.

22. Unpublished, except for a few passages; private collection.

23. Fragment of a letter published by Denis de Rougemont, *Icare*, no. 96, p. 23.

24. It proved impossible to trace this document, which was shown at the Bibliothèque Nationale in 1951 (papers of Consuelo de Saint-Exupéry).

25. Unpublished; private collection.

1944

1. *Lettres à sa mère*, p. 170.

2. Unpublished; private collection.

3. See *Icare*, no. 96, p. 74, "Que faire de Saint-Ex?" (letter from General Bouscat to André Le Troquer, Commissioner for War and the Air Force); see also Cate, p. 497.

4. Published in Pélissier, p. 153.

5. Ibid., p. 154.

6. Ibid., pp. 154–5.

7. Ibid., p. 152.

8. Unpublished; from the original, kindly provided by Mme François de Rose.

9. Carbon copy of the original; private collection. Excerpted in Chevrier, 1949, pp. 243–5 (dated "December 1943" and entitled "Letter to General Z"); also in *Icare*, no. 96, p. 53. General Diégo-Charles-Joseph Brosset was commander of the First Free French Division.

10. Published in Pélissier, pp. 47–8; written on letterhead of the Residency of France in Tunisia.

11. *Lettres à sa mère*, p. 171.

12. Pierre Dalloz, pp. 272–4; excerpted in Chevrier, 1958, pp. 188–9. Reprinted several times; for a facsimile, see Dalloz, "Destins unis: Saint-Exupéry et Jean Prévost," *Icare*, no. 96, pp. 169–73.

13. Gavoille, "D'Alghero à Borgo," *Icare*, no. 96, pp. 97–102.

14. V. F. Robison, "Avec les français," *Icare*, no. 96, p. 115.

15. Chevrier, 1949, pp. 280–3.
16. Published by Hans Martin in the journal *Der Landser*, no. 725 (1972). We wish to thank the publishers, Erich Pabel of Rastatt, for their kind permission to reprint this text.
17. Published in the first *Cahier Saint-Exupéry*, 1980, pp. 62–4. See also Gavoille, "D'Alghero à Borgo," *Icare*, no. 96, p. 101.

Index

INDEX